Agricultural Finance in India

The Role of NABARD

K. Prabhakar Rajkumar

NEW NC CENTURY

New Century Publications
New Delhi, India

NEW CENTURY PUBLICATIONS
4852 / 24, 1st Floor,
Ansari Road, Daryaganj,
New Delhi – 110 002 (India)

Tel.: 011-4101 7798; 4358 7398; 98112 66355
E-mail: info@newcenturypublications.com

www.newcenturypublications.com

Editorial office:
4800 / 24, Bharat Ram Road,
Ansari Road, Daryaganj,
New Delhi – 110 002

Edition: 2024

ISBN: **978-81-7708-180-0**

First Published: July 2008

Published by New Century Publications and printed at Milan Enterprises, New Delhi.

Designs: Patch Creative Unit, New Delhi.

PRINTED IN INDIA

Foreword

Indian agriculture was backward and stagnant at the time of Independence in 1947. Ever since the launching of the First Five Year Plan (1951-52 to 1955-56), agricultural sector has received the prime attention of the Government in the overall strategy of economic development. As a result, farm productivity has increased over the years and the country has achieved high degree of self-sufficiency in terms of foodgrains and raw material for agro-based industries. The breakthrough in agriculture has been achieved as a result of substantial public investment in irrigation, agricultural research and extension schemes, subsidised inputs, credit facilities and price support programmes.

I am pleased to learn about the forthcoming book of Dr. K. Prabhakar Rajkumar under the titled *Agricultural Finance in India: The Role of NABARD.* The work is a timely contribution to the existing body of literature on Indian agriculture. It assumes added significance at a time when Central and State Governments are making all out efforts to usher India in a second green revolution. The book deals with the system of agricultural finance in India and makes a detailed analysis of the role of National Bank for Agriculture and Rural Development (NABARD) in this context. The latest information given about the organisational structure of NABARD and its refinance activities will provide useful insights to all those interested in agricultural developments in India. I commend Dr. Rajkumar on the excellent work accomplished by him.

June 17, 2008

M. Thangaraju
Vice-chancellor, Periyar University
Salem, Tamil Nadu, India

ABOUT THE BOOK

Agricultural production in India depends upon millions of small farmers. It is the intensity of their effort and the efficiency of their technique that will help in raising yields per acre. Because of inadequate financial resources and absence of timely credit facilities at reasonable rates, many of the farmers, even though otherwise willing, are unable to go in for improved seeds and manures or to introduce better methods or techniques. It is, therefore, of the utmost importance that the financial requirements of the farmers are adequately met.

Till Independence in 1947, money lenders and the landlords were the principal sources of rural credit. Over the years, the operations of moneylenders have declined in view of debt relief legislations, the system of licensing moneylenders and restrictions on the use and transfer of land as security. Similarly, the abolition of all privileged tenures both in zamindari and ryotwari areas has discouraged investment by the landlords and larger cultivators.

Provision of sufficient and timely credit at fair rates of interest has, therefore, to be considered as an integral part of agricultural development. Assistance rendered by way of credit has, however, to be related to specific items of productive work or of essential costs of cultivation.

Set up in 1982, National Bank for Agriculture and Rural Development (NABARD) is the apex institution accredited with all matters concerning policy, planning and operations in the field of credit for agriculture and other economic activities in rural areas in India. NABARD serves as an apex refinancing agency for the institutions providing investment and production credit in rural areas.

This book explains the system of agricultural finance in India. It provides an in-depth analysis of the role of NABARD as the apex refinance body, in promoting agricultural and rural development in India.

ABOUT THE AUTHOR

Dr. K. Prabhakar Rajkumar M. Com., M.Phil., M.B.A., Ph.D. is lecturer in the Department of Commerce, Periyar University, Salem. He specialises in banking, finance and accounting. He has published 45 research articles in national level journals and 6 research articles in international journals. He has successfully completed one Major Research Project funded by University Grants Commission (UGC), New Delhi. He is a member of Advisory and Editorial Board of *Economic Challenger*, a refereed journal of India.

PREFACE

The largest portion of the natural resources of India consists of land and by far the largest number of its inhabitants is engaged in agriculture. Therefore in any scheme of economic development of the country, agriculture holds a position of basic importance. Agricultural sector occupies a key position in the Indian economy. It provides employment to about 65 per cent of the working population of India. Around one-quarter of India's national income originates from the agricultural sector. It is imperative that the problems of farmers are addressed with a sense of urgency. Agriculture being a State subject, the bulk of public investment in agriculture takes place at the level of States and the Central Government supports the States as a catalyst.

Agricultural production in India depends upon millions of small farmers. It is the intensity of their effort and the efficiency of their technique that will help in raising yields per acre. Because of inadequate financial resources and absence of timely credit facilities at reasonable rates, many of the farmers, even though otherwise willing, are unable to go in for improved seeds and manures or to introduce better methods or techniques. It is, therefore, of the utmost importance that the financial requirements of the farmers are adequately met.

Till Independence in 1947, money lenders and the landlords were the principal sources of rural credit. Over the years, the operations of moneylenders have declined in view of debt relief legislations, the system of licensing moneylenders and restrictions on the use and transfer of land as security. Similarly, the abolition of all privileged tenures both in zamindari and ryotwari areas has discouraged investment by the landlords and larger cultivators.

Provision of sufficient and timely credit at fair rates of interest has, therefore, to be considered as an integral part of agricultural development. Assistance rendered by way of credit has, however, to be related to specific items of productive work or of essential costs of cultivation.

Agricultural growth is crucial for alleviating rural poverty. Access to institutional credit to more farmers and appropriate quantity and quality of agricultural credit are crucial for realising the full potential of agriculture as a profitable activity.

Set up in 1982, National Bank for Agriculture and Rural Development (NABARD) is the apex institution accredited with all matters concerning policy, planning and operations in the field of credit for agriculture and other economic activities in rural areas in India. NABARD serves as an apex refinancing agency for the institutions providing investment and production credit in rural areas.

Other main activities of NABARD include (a) initiating measures towards institution building for improving absorptive capacity of the credit delivery system, including monitoring, formulation of rehabilitation schemes, restructuring of credit institutions and training of personnel, (b) co-ordinating the rural financing activities of all institutions engaged in developmental work at the field level (c) maintaining liaison with the Government of India, the State Governments, the RBI and other national level institutions concerned with policy formulation and (d) undertaking monitoring and evaluation of projects refinanced by it.

This book explains the system of agricultural finance in India. It provides an in-depth analysis of the role of NABARD as the apex refinance body, in promoting agricultural and rural development in India.

The work, it is hoped, will provide useful insight and material to all those interested in Indian agriculture. Thanks are due to Mr. Sandeep Sury, New Century Publications, New Delhi, for bringing out this book in a very short span of time.

June 2008 **Dr. K. Prabhakar Rajkumar**
Salem, Tamil Nadu

CONTENTS

1

Indian Agriculture: An Overview

1.1 Role of Agriculture: Conflicting Views

In almost all developing countries, agriculture plays a predominant role in shaping and moulding the lives of people to a great extent. In fact agriculture is the basic industry viewed as a way of life as far as these people are concerned and that it has never been viewed by them in the narrow sense of business-producing, retailing, purchasing, profit making and so on. It is true that man does not live by food alone. But without food, which he derives from agriculture, man cannot exist at all and on that existence only rests his ability to enjoy many other comforts of life. Experts do differ in their views regarding the role of agriculture in shaping the society. But one thing is certain: agriculture beckons man back to nature and tries to keep him there, which is ecologically more beneficial whereas, modern industry forces man to lead a kind of life, which is artificial and devoid of the soothing caresses of Mother Nature.

There have been orthodox thinkers like Bakers, Wilson Barsodi and Humphries who view agriculture as the fundamental and most basic industry. Their views are based on the fact that it is agriculture which feeds the human race and hence it is the basis of the existence of Homo sapiens. The orthodox thinkers came to the conclusion that if agriculture ceases to support and sustain the social structure, all other aspects which too support civilization would collapse. But the modern thinkers adopt a different outlook challenging the assumptions of the orthodox thinkers. The most famous representative of the group of modern thinkers is J.S. Davis who argues that wealth and welfare of nations depend upon many complex conditions. In modern times, agriculture is not uniquely basic, and the prosperity of a nation depends largely on factors other than the work of those who till the soil.

Between these two extreme views, there are also some other thinkers who take a balanced view of things. Karl Brandt, H.R. Tolley and P. Chew belong to this middle-of-the course point of view. They made a study of the agricultural and industrial communities both in the East and the West, and concluded that agriculture as well as other sectors of economy enjoys equal importance. They based their argument on the analogy of the whole body feeling the pain, even if only one limb is affected. In other words, one part of the country depending on agriculture cannot be happy and prosperous, if another part supported by industrial enterprises is in distress, and vice versa.

Some writers like, W.F. Gwen, Ranger Nurkse, P.N. Rosenstein Rondan, T.A. Scitovsky and Arthur W. Lewis suggested a balanced growth approach giving equal priority to both, the farm and non-farm sectors for healthy economic progress. Lewis recommended an approach based on balanced growth of both agricultural and industrial sectors and treating them both as equally important. Economists like T.W. Schultz, W.W. Rostow and Simon Kuznets held the view that, if we aspired for the development of the industrial sector as well as for the overall development of economy, then the transformation of agriculture would become unavoidable.

According to Simon Kuznets if agriculture itself grows, it makes a product contribution; if it trades with others, it renders a market contribution; if it transfers resources to other sectors, these resources being productive factors, it makes a factor contribution. Indian economists like C.N. Vakil and P.R. Brahmanand warn against concentrating all our energies on industry only. They have opined that a determined persistence in expansion of the fixed-capital to the neglect of expansion of wage goods (food grains) will land the economy in a ridiculous state in which there would tend to be unemployment of labour as well as equipment with no possible escape out of it.

1.2 Importance of Agriculture in the Indian Economy

The largest portion of the natural resources of India consists of land and by far the largest number of its inhabitants is engaged in agriculture. Therefore in any scheme of economic development of the country, agriculture holds a position of basic importance. Although Indian agriculture is way back compared to the levels in developed countries, some notable developments have occurred over the years since Independence in 1947. Large areas which suffered from repeated failures of rainfall have received irrigation; new crops have come to occupy a significant position in the country's production and trade; the agricultural and the industrial economies in the country now exert a powerful influence on one another; problems of rural indebtedness and the exploitative practices of the village moneylender are much less, and finally there is already in the countryside an awakening and a desire for raising standards of living.

Agricultural sector occupies a key position in the Indian economy. It provides employment to about 65 per cent of the working population of India. Around one-quarter of India's national income originates from the agricultural sector. It is imperative that the problems of farmers are addressed with a sense of urgency. Agriculture being a State subject, the bulk of public investment in agriculture takes place at the level of States and the Central Government supports the States as a catalyst.

The First Five Year Plan (1951-56) accorded the highest priority to the agricultural sector to tide over the difficult food problem created by the partition of the country. Agriculture has occupied an important place in every successive plan. Two major components of agricultural development strategy have been: (a) subsidies on inputs and (b) minimum support price for output.

Agricultural products like cereals (mainly rice), tea, coffee, cashew, spices, tobacco and leather are important items of India's exports and hence foreign exchange earnings.

Agriculture is also the source of raw material for agro-based industries including textiles, cigarettes, jute, sugar, paper, processed foodstuffs and *vanaspati*. Moreover, agricultural sector provides market for capital goods (tractors, pump sets and other agricultural machinery), inputs (fertilisers, insecticides), and light consumer goods. The nation has invested huge resources for the development of agriculture under various plans.

The development of the agricultural sector depends, to a large extent, on such core industries as power, petroleum, fertilisers and machine tools. Thus, there is inter-dependence between agriculture and industry.

1.3 Cropping Pattern in Indian Agriculture

Cropping pattern refers to the distribution of cultivated land among different crops grown in a country. Cropping pattern reveals the nature of agricultural operations, e.g. the importance of food crops vis-à-vis cash crops. Cropping pattern is influenced by a host of factors which can be broadly classified into two categories: (a) physical factors and (b) economic factors.

Among the physical factors, the important ones are soil conditions, extent of rainfall and type of climate. The economic factors include relative prices of agricultural commodities, size of the farms, availability of inputs, demand conditions, system of land holding and government policy regarding exports, imports, taxes and subsidies.

There are two main agricultural seasons in India: (a) *kharif* under which crops are planted at the onset of the Southwest monsoon in June-July and harvested in September-October, (b) *rabi* under which crops are planted usually between October and December and harvested between March and May. Major *kharif* crops are rice, jowar, bajra, maize, cotton, sugarcane, soyabean and groundnut. Major *rabi* crops are wheat, barley, gram, linseed, rapeseed and mustard.

India is a large country with diverse climatic, soil and

terrain conditions. Therefore, a wide variety of crops are grown.

1. Foodgrains: These include rice, wheat, coarse cereals (like maize, gram, *bajra, jowar)*, and pulses. These crops constitute the backbone of India's food economy. In India, nearly 75 per cent of the cultivated area is occupied by food crops including rice, wheat, millets and pulses. Paddy (rice) is the most important food crop in India followed by wheat. There has been no significant change in the cropping pattern during the post-Independence period. The present cropping pattern is unbalanced as it is heavily tilted in favour of paddy and wheat while area under oilseeds and pulses is less than required.
2. Oilseeds: There are ten major oilseeds produced in India, namely groundnut, castorseed, sesame, nigerseed, soyabean, sunflower, rapeseed, mustard, linseed and safflower. Of these, groundnut, rapeseed, mustard and soyabean occupy commanding position in terms of total production.
3. Fibre Crops: Cotton and jute are the chief crops under this category.
4. Plantation Crops: Sugarcane, tea, coffee, tobacco, rubber, cocoa, cardamom, cashew and coconut. Some of these crops constitute important items of India's exports. India is the largest producer, processor, consumer and exporter of cashew in the world. Coconut is an important tree crop grown extensively in coastal areas providing livelihood to about 10 million people in cultivation, processing and related activities.
5. Horticultural Crops: India, with its wide variability of climate and soil, produces a large range of horticultural crops such as fruits, vegetables, potato, tropical tuber crops, ornamental crops, medicinal and aromatic plants, spices (like black pepper, cardamom, ginger, garlic, turmeric, chillies). The National Horticulture Mission was launched on April 1, 2005. The Mission will ensure end-

to-end approach having backward and forward linkages covering research, production, post-harvest management, processing and marketing. Indian agriculture has indeed diversified from foodgrains to a variety of crops but more needs to be done in this regard. In his 2005-06 budget speech, the Finance Minister announced the preparation of a roadmap by the Ministry of Agriculture. The roadmap will focus on fruits, vegetables, flowers, dairy, poultry, fisheries, pulses and oilseeds.

1.4 Small-sized Agricultural Holdings

Small-sized holdings are a disturbing feature of the Indian agriculture. The average size of farms has become smaller over the years and the trend continues. An important reason for this trend is the growth of population which has adversely affected the per capita availability of land.

The pressure of population along with some social and economic factors has decreased the size of agricultural holdings in India. Various surveys conducted by official agencies point out this fact. There are various reasons for sub-division and fragmentation of holdings in India.

The laws of inheritance in India give to all children an equal share in the property of their parents. After the enactment of the Hindu Code Bill, daughters have also become, along with sons, entitled to an equal share in the property of their parents. Consequently, land is being sub-divided with every passing generation.

Decline of joint family system has also contributed to the break-up of agricultural holdings. Legal heirs prefer to have their individual shares in family property instead of holding it as joint property of the family. The rise of individualism in modern societies has hastened the decline of joint family system.

Rural indebtedness has also contributed to the sub-division and fragmentation of holdings. As is well known, most farmers in India are indebted to moneylenders and landlords. In the event of non-payment of their debt, they are forced to sell a portion of their land to the creditor.

It is a common practice in India to lease out land to tenants on crop-sharing basis. Quite often the landlords lease out their land to a number of tenants to avoid trouble and also to circumvent the land laws. Due to these practices, land gets sub-divided and fragmented.

Sub-division of holdings leads to loss of cultivable land due to boundaries. Too many boundaries cause disputes, often leading to litigation. Instead of investing their precious resources in improving the productivity of land, farmers waste their limited funds in settling claims and counter claims. This tendency has created tensions in rural areas.

Fragmented holdings create difficulties in the management of land resources. When a farmer has to shift from one piece of land to another, it involves wastage of manpower and extra expenses. Similarly, small-sized farms restrict opportunities for the use of modern science and technology. Proper arrangements for irrigation cannot be made if farms belonging to a farmer are scattered here and there. Modern agricultural machines cannot be successfully operated on tiny farms. Absence or limited use of modern agricultural practices keeps farm productivity low.

1.5 Low Productivity of Indian Agriculture

Indian agriculture was backward and stagnant at the time of Independence. Ever since the launching of the First Five Year Plan (1951-56), agricultural sector has received the prime attention of the Government in the overall strategy of economic development. As a result, farm productivity has increased over the years and the country has achieved high degree of self-sufficiency in terms of foodgrains and raw material for agro-based industries.

Although per hectare yield of major crops has increased over the last four decades yet it is far below the international levels. This scenario calls for an examination of the causes of low productivity of agriculture in India.

1.5.1 Causes of Low Productivity: Statistical evidence suggests that farm productivity in India is low as compared to other countries of the world. The low productivity of the agricultural sector is attributable to a host of technological and institutional factors. Some of the important of these factors are described below.

A. Technological Factors: These include the following.

Lack of Irrigation Facilities: Despite best efforts during the last five decades, only one-third of cultivated land has the facility of artificial irrigation. In other words, most of the farmers depend on uncertain rainfall for irrigation of their fields. Rainfall is uncertain in terms of quantity, place and time. Agriculture is still a gamble in monsoon for millions of farmers in this country.

Limited Use of Fertilisers: Adequate use of fertilisers is crucial for improving the farm productivity. Unfortunately, the use of fertilisers by Indian farmers is much below the level achieved in developed countries.

Limited Use of High Yield Variety of Seeds: The HYV programme was started in 1966. The percentage of HYV area to total area differs from crop to crop. In the case of wheat it is quite high. However, the coverage of area under HYV for other crops is relatively low.

Inadequate Plant Protection Schemes: Another reason for low productivity is the damage caused to crops by insects, pests, and plant diseases. The use of pesticides and insecticides is not widespread, particularly among the small and marginal farmers. Central Integrated Pest Management Centres have been set up in various States to monitor crop pests, and to organise training in pest management for extension workers and farmers.

Lack of Farm Mechanisation: Most Indian farmers still use age-old farming techniques like wooden plough, cattle power, and sickle. The use of modern farm machinery is limited to affluent farmers in selected regions of the country.

There is a great deal of controversy regarding mechanisation of agriculture in view of widespread unemployment and disguised unemployment in rural areas. Therefore, the policy regarding mechanisation of agriculture has to be cautious and selective.

Floods and Soil Erosion: Floods are a common occurrence in one or the other part of the country every year. The consequent soil erosion and waterlogging dislocates production cycle, resulting in loss of agricultural output.

1.5.2 Institutional Factors: Use of modern methods of production is conditioned by the institutional framework of a production sector. If the institutional set up is exploitative, it will discourage the adoption of efficient technology. Unfortunately, the institutional setting of the farm sector in India is not congenial for the use of modern agricultural technology.

Feudal Land Relations: Although *zamindari* system was abolished soon after Independence, it continues to exist in a different garb. Land reform laws have proved ineffective and therefore big landlords still rule the roost in rural areas. They lease out their land to tenants and charge high rents. The various tenancy malpractices hardly provide any incentive to tenant farmers to improve land and productivity.

Small-sized Holdings: As a result of population growth, there is tremendous pressure on available cultivable land. This has led to overcrowding and hence sub-division and fragmentation of holdings. Small-sized and scattered holdings imply wastage of time and labour, difficulties in the use of modern techniques, and quarrels and litigation among farmers. The existence of these problems is also responsible for poor farm yield.

Rural Indebtedness: Poverty of the Indian farmer forces him to borrow money for his existence. The institution of money lending is the greatest curse for the poor and illiterate rural folk of India. Although the importance of moneylenders has declined over the last 55 years, they are still very dominant in providing credit to the farmers. The exploitative practices of the moneylenders are no secret. Their malpractices include charging of high rate of interest and adopting unfair means in the maintenance of accounts.

Marketing Difficulties: Marketing is the last ring in the production chain. If the marketing system is inefficient and denies the farmers a reasonable return for their efforts, they will be discouraged to produce more. Unfortunately, the present marketing system of agricultural produce is not favourable to the interests of the farmers. The preponderance of intermediaries and the malpractices of commission agents deny remunerative prices to the farmers.

Thus, low productivity in Indian agriculture is the result of a number of technological and institutional factors which influence each other. The causes of low agricultural productivity explained above suggest their own remedies.

Over the years, however, the share of agriculture in GDP has fallen significantly and, as a result, the aggregate GDP has become relatively less sensitive to fluctuations in agricultural performance. This factor is of course well recognised, but the role of agriculture, and particularly agricultural incomes, in influencing GDP growth indirectly through the demand side is less well understood. Table 1.1 presents the share of agriculture in GDP and the share of non-food consumption in rural expenditures over the last three decades.

Table 1.1: Declining Share of Agriculture in GDP (per cent)

Year	Share of agriculture in GDP	Share of non-food in rural expenditures
1973-74	44.0	25.1
1983	38.7	34.4
1993-94	32.9	36.8
1999-2000	26.9	40.6

Source: Government of India, Planning Commission, *Tenth Five Year Plan* (2002-07), Vol. I, p. 28.

As can be seen, while the share of agriculture in GDP has fallen from 44 per cent in 1973-74 to 27 per cent in 1999-2000, non-food expenditure has risen from 25 per cent in 1973-74 to nearly 41 per cent in 1999-2000. In other words, a 1 per cent change in the growth rate of agriculture would have affected the GDP growth rate by 0.44 per cent in 1973-74 but only by 0.27 per cent in 1999-2000. On the other hand, the indirect effects of change in agricultural growth through the demand for non-agricultural goods and services has actually gone up from a little under 12 per cent of total aggregate demand in 1973-74 to nearly 14 per cent in 1999-2000. In the future, as average agricultural incomes increase, this indirect effect of agricultural incomes on non-agricultural growth will become progressively stronger as the bulk of the incremental income in rural areas will be spent on non-agricultural goods and services and not on food.

1.6 Marketing of Agricultural Produce

The disposal of the produce after the harvest and the return obtained has a significant effect on production and on the welfare of the cultivator. Production in agriculture being seasonal, the crop is harvested during a short period and consumed gradually. While commodities like cotton and groundnut require large storage space which the average cultivator lacks, fruits, vegetables and sugarcane are of a perishable nature. The farmer has, therefore, to dispose of his surplus immediately either at the village or at the *mandi.* In the absence of staying power of a large number of small farmers, they compete with each other and the markets witness conditions of occasional glut and scarcity. A major part of the commercial crops like cotton, jute, sugarcane and oilseeds has to be marketed immediately as the farmers are in need of cash for meeting their dues and other expenses. As regards foodgrains the marketable surplus varies by crops and regions. The total quantity and value of the marketed produce, even in a predominantly subsistence economy as in India is considerable.

Sale of agricultural produce involves a number of functions such as assembling, storing, grading, standardising, transporting and financing the produce and negotiating sale. Some of these operations may be performed by the farmer, but storage and sale of a commodity and finding finance for purchase, call for specialised knowledge and adequate resources which the individual cultivator does not possess.

The village money lender or the *mandi arhatiya* advances loans to farmers for securing production requirements like seeds, and manures and for meeting other needs. These debts some times carry an understanding or an obligation to sell the produce to or through the lender or his nominee. At the time of sale the position of advantage occupied by the village banker gets reflected either in a lower price or unfair weights or delayed settlement. If the sale takes place in the *mandi* or the market through the brokers or *arhatiyas* the farmer pays not only for the services rendered by the middlemen but is also subjected to other unwarranted deductions.

The benefits of a regulated market which attempt only to improve the existing practices are limited; without changing the marketing structure the number of middlemen and costs cannot be reduced. Efforts in this direction have been made in some States by organising cooperative marketing. The progress of marketing societies, in spite of immense scope, has so far been slow. The entry of a co-operative even as an agent is not generally favoured by the trade.

1.6.1 Present System of Marketing: Marketing is the last link in the chain of production process. An efficient marketing system which ensures reasonable return to the producers is essential to induce them to produce more.

During the pre-Independence period, Indian agriculture was backward and stagnant and there was hardly any marketable surplus. Therefore, the system of marketing, though defective, did not attract much attention. However, in the post-Independence period and particularly after the green revolution, agricultural marketing has become a prime concern for the planners. Due to increase in agricultural productivity, the marketable surplus has increased, necessitating reforms in the existing system. The objectives of these reforms are to ensure (a) fair prices for the produce of the farmers, (b) adequate and regular availability of foodgrains for urban areas and (c) regular supplies of raw materials for the industries.

Various systems of agricultural marketing exist in India. An important traditional system is the sale of produce to moneylenders and village traders. This system is closely related to the problem of rural indebtedness. Farmers who are indebted to moneylenders are forced to sell their produce to them. It is understandable that the price paid by the moneylenders is considerably lower than the market price.

Another traditional practice is the sale of produce in the *hats* and *shandies*. *Hats* are village markets held once or twice a week and serve a small cluster of villages. *Shandies* are also village markets held at longer intervals or on special occasions.

An important component of the marketing system is the widespread network of regulated wholesale markets. These markets are generally located near or in a township and serve a number of surrounding villages. The farmers sell their produce to the commission agents with the help of brokers. It is well-known that various types of malpractices exist in these markets, e.g. use of wrong measures and weights. *Hats* and *shandies* constitute, for a great majority of farmers in India, particularly the small producers, the focal points for disposal of farm produce as well as sale and purchase centres for non-agricultural products.

Involvement of government agencies with the marketing of agricultural produce is a welcome development. Co-operative societies and government agencies have helped the farmers to escape the exploitative practices of the private dealers. Leading agencies involved in procurement and support price operations on behalf of the Government are: Food Corporation of India, Cotton Corporation of India, Jute

Corporation of India and the Co-operatives with National Agricultural Co-operative Marketing Federation (NAFED) as their apex organisation.

From time to time, Government announces procurement or minimum support prices for various agricultural crops.

1.6.2 Measures to Improve Agricultural Marketing: Defects in the present system of agricultural marketing can be removed by providing the following facilities to the farmers.

- In view of the poverty of the Indian farmers, it is necessary to provide them with credit facilities at the time of harvest so that they are not forced to sell their produce at that time. Soon after the harvest, the prices of agricultural products are relatively low. Farmers should have the choice to wait for better times, i.e. better prices. This can be done by providing them with short-term credit to build their staying power.
- If the farmers decide to postpone the sale of their produce in view of low prices at the time of harvest, they should have proper warehousing facilities. Government should provide scientific storage facilities at reasonable charges in or near the villages. This task can be entrusted to the Central Warehousing Corporation and the State Warehousing Corporations.
- Next in logical order are the transport facilities. Villages in India are not well connected with cities and townships through *pucca* roads or railways. If efficient transport facilities are available to farmers throughout the year, they can take their produce to markets of their choice to secure remunerative prices.
- It is also necessary to provide adequate and latest information to the farmers regarding prices of various agricultural commodities prevailing in different markets. Although this is being done through radio and television, there is the need to extend the coverage of these facilities to all parts of the country.
- Farmers should be provided with reasonable amenities in

the *mandies*. Efforts should be made to reduce the presence of large number of middlemen in the *mandies* who erode profits of the farmers considerably. Arrangements should exist for grading and standardisation of agricultural produce. Moreover, provision should be made for following facilities in the *mandies,* viz. post office, banking, lodging and boarding for overnight stay and parking for vehicles.

Improvement in the marketing system will go a long way to ensure remunerative prices to the farmers, inducing them to produce more.

1.6.3 Inter-Ministerial Task Force on Agricultural Marketing: The Inter-Ministerial Task Force set up by the Ministry of Agriculture to strengthen and develop agricultural marketing submitted its Report in June 2002, outlining several reforms in agricultural marketing. It recommended amendment to the States' Agricultural Produce Marketing Acts for promotion of direct marketing and contract farming, development of agricultural markets in private and cooperative sectors, stepping up of pledge financing, expansion of futures trading to cover all agricultural commodities, introduction of negotiable warehousing receipt system and use of information technology to provide market led extension services to farmers. At a National Conference on Agriculture Marketing Reforms organized by the Ministry of Agriculture on 27th September 2002 in New Delhi, all the State Governments and Union Territory Administrations were requested to implement the reforms measures by bringing out suitable amendments in the existing state legislation. A Committee of State Ministers has also been set up under the Chairmanship of Union Minister of State (Agriculture) to accelerate the implementation of the reform measures.

1.6.4 Salient Features of the Model Act for State Agricultural Produce Marketing (Development and Regulation) Act, 2003: Marketing of agricultural produce is the most important activity for the farming community, particularly for those who are small producers and have small surpluses for marketing. To protect the interests of farmers, Government promoted organized marketing of agricultural commodities through a network of regulated markets. However, studies indicate that the institutions of regulated markets have achieved limited success, as these markets restricted development of direct and free marketing, smooth raw material supplied to agro-processors, information exchange and adoption of innovative marketing systems and technologies.

To benefit the farming community from new market access opportunities, the internal agricultural marketing system in the country needs to be integrated and strengthened. In this context, an inter-Ministerial Task Force set up by the Ministry of Agriculture suggested a package of reform measures, such as amendments in the States' Agricultural Produce Marketing Acts to encourage development of competitive agricultural markets in the private and cooperative sectors, and deregulation of marketing system to promote private investment in marketing infrastructure.

The Department of Agriculture and Cooperation has formulated a model law on agricultural marketing and contract farming in consultation with the State Governments and representatives of trade and industry. The salient features of the model law are given below.

- Legal persons, growers and local authorities permitted to establish new markets in any area.
- No compulsion on growers to sell their produce through existing regulated markets.
- Establishment of direct purchase centers, Consumers/Farmers Markets for direct sale.
- Promotion of Public-Private Partnership in the management and development of agricultural markets.
- Separate constitution of special markets for commodities like onions, fruits, vegetables, and flowers.
- A separate chapter to regulate and promote contract-

farming arrangements in the country.

- Prohibition of commission agency in any transaction of agricultural commodities with the producers.
- Market Committee to promote alternative marketing system, contract farming, direct marketing and farmers/consumers markets.
- State Marketing Boards to promote standardization, grading, quality certification, market led extension and training of farmers and market functionaries in marketing related areas.
- Constitution of State Marketing Standards Bureau for promotion of grading, standardization and quality certification of agricultural produce.

1.6.5 Commodity Futures and Agricultural Marketing: The country, as at end-March 2006, was served with 7,566 regulated and 21,780 rural primary/periodic agricultural markets. On an average, 21 villages were served by one rural market. While every village in Kerala has a market, in Himachal Pradesh, 667 villages on an average were served by one market. Model Act formulated by the Ministry of Agriculture to inspire marketing reforms to meet the emerging demand, enables public private partnership, contract farming, and establishment of private markets and direct purchase centers. In an effort to improve agricultural marketing, 15 State Governments and 5 Union Territories (UTs) have amended their Agricultural Produce Marketing Committee Act to meet the requirements and to take advantage of the liberalized and globalised economy.

Various private initiatives due to developments in Information and Communication Technology (ICT) have further improved agricultural marketing. As at end-December 2006, 94 commodities were traded in the commodity futures market, including major agricultural commodities. Trade in commodity derivatives increased from Rs. 1.29 lakh crore during 2003-04 to Rs. 27.39 lakh crore during 2006 (April-December). Of the total transactions, 59 and 34 per cent were shared by the Multi-Commodity Exchange and the National Commodity Derivatives Exchange, Mumbai, respectively.

1.7 New Agricultural Strategy/Green Revolution

The mid-1960s was a landmark in the history of Indian agriculture. It was in 1966 that a New Agricultural Strategy was put into practice to tide over the chronic shortages of foodgrains in the country. This strategy was called High-Yielding Varieties Programme (HYVP), popularly known as Green Revolution.

The response to the food crisis of the late 1960s was to promote the green revolution in rice and wheat through the provision of a package providing research and extension services, inputs like improved seeds, fertiliser and irrigation and assured off take through MSP based public procurement. This has been implemented successfully over the past 40 years. However, with mounting foodstocks this strategy for agricultural growth has now played itself out.

1.7.1 Scope and Achievements of High Yielding Variety (HYV) Programme: The HYV programme was initially launched in certain selected districts of the country as, for example, Ludhiana in Punjab, Aligarh in Uttar Pradesh, and West Godavari in Andhra Pradesh. Later on, it was extended to many more districts in different States. The HYV programme concentrated mainly on wheat and paddy, the two important cereals of the food basket. The HYV programme consisted of a package which included regular and adequate irrigation facilities, use of fertilisers, better quality seeds, pesticides and insecticides.

The need to increase foodgrains production was so urgent that the HYV Programme was implemented in suitable areas with the help of farmers who could afford the package deal. The Government had to grow more food as quickly as possible, irrespective of where it was grown and by whom.

The results of the adoption of the HYV Programme were quick and substantial. Foodgrains production which had hovered around 50-60 million tonnes per year since 1950-51 started increasing at a fast rate (Table 1.2). The main achievement was in the area of wheat production and therefore many economists called it wheat revolution instead of green revolution.

Table 1.2: Foodgrains Production in India: 1950-51 to 2006-07

Year	Production (million tonne)
1050-51	50.8
1960-61	82.0
1970-71	108.4
1980-81	129.6
1990-91	176.4
2001-02	212.9
2002-03	174.8
2003-04	213.2
2004-05	198.4
2005-06	208.6
2006-07	209.2

Source: Government of India, *Economic Survey*, 2000-2001, p. 153, Tables 8.5 and 8.6 and *Economic Survey*, 2006-07, p. 161, Table 8.6.

Broadly speaking, foodgrains production has recorded a four-fold increase over a period of half a century. However, the increase in per capita availability of foodgrains per day has been modest: from 395 grams in 1951 to 422 grams in 2005. This is attributable to the enormous increase in population over the same period. The increase in foodgrains production has helped the country to achieve considerable degree of self-sufficiency in terms of food requirements and tide over recurring food shortages reminiscent of the 1960s and 1970s. The breakthrough has been achieved as a result of substantial public investment in irrigation, agricultural research and extension schemes, subsidised inputs, credit facilities and price support programmes.

Lauding the achievements of Indian agriculture, the *Economic Survey*, 2000-2001 observed, "Technology led development in agriculture has made India self-sufficient in foodgrains and a leading producer of several agricultural commodities in the world. The **green revolution** in crops, **yellow revolution** in oilseeds, **white revolution** in milk production, **blue revolution** in fish production and **golden revolution** in horticulture bear an ample testimony to the contributions of agricultural research and development efforts undertaken in the country." [1]

Foodgrains production will have to be stepped up in the coming years in view of the increasing population. In this connection, Reserve Bank of India's *Report on Currency and Finance* (1998-99) has observed, "Although the country has become self-sufficient in food production, the country needs to produce large quantities than at present to keep pace with the ever-increasing population. It is estimated by the Planning Commission that the country needs to produce about 300 million tonnes of foodgrains by 2011-12, an increase of almost 100 million tonnes in less than a decade and a half." [2]

However, further increase in foodgrains production is becoming difficult. According to Government of India's *Economic Survey*, 1999-2000, "There are limits to increasing production through area expansion as the country has almost reached a plateau in so far as cultivable land is concerned. Hence the emphasis has to be on increasing productivity levels. The area under foodgrains has more or less remained constant at around 125 million hectares since 1970-71." [3]

1.7.2 Problems Created by Green Revolution: Although the New Agricultural Strategy has helped to tide over the food problem to a considerable extent, it has not been a happy experience altogether. Instead, it has left in its trail a variety of inequalities which have caused socio-politico tensions.

A. Inter-regional Inequalities: To ensure that benefits of development planning flow to all parts of the country, regional balanced development has all along been accepted as an important objective of economic planning in India. However, the pattern of agricultural development over the years has not promoted this cherished objective of Five Year Plans. As the Seventh Five Year Plan (1985-90) observed, "Another feature of agricultural performance is that the bulk of increase in output particularly foodgrains, has been concentrated in a few regions which are well-endowed with infrastructure like surface irrigation, rural electrification, roads and markets and where farmers are resourceful in terms of their capacity to invest and bear risks. The favourable institutional framework in such areas is also responsible for the initiative and drive displayed by the farmers. It has been estimated that such developed areas accounting for less than 15 per cent of the area under foodgrains in the country contributed as much as 56 per cent of the increase in foodgrains production in the post-green revolution period." [4] Regional disparities, far from being lessened, have actually increased.

From the very beginning, the HYV Programme was directed to those regions which possessed proper irrigation facilities and were not prone to natural calamities such as floods and droughts. These were precisely the regions which were relatively developed and could afford to purchase the inputs included in the package. Naturally, the bulk of increase in output remained concentrated in a few regions, particularly Punjab, Haryana and Western Uttar Pradesh. Eighth Five Year Plan (1992-97), noting with concern the striking regional and crop imbalances observed, "The benefits of Green Revolution which remain confined at present to the north and north-west, must spread to other regions, more particularly to the eastern and north-eastern region, which have adequate rainfall, fertile soil and unlimited scope for stepping up agricultural production." [5]

Thus, the new agricultural strategy has worked against the nationally accepted objective of regional balanced development.

B. Inter-personal Inequalities: Since the new agricultural strategy required assured irrigation facilities, it remained confined mostly to big farmers. The new technology is beyond the means of the small and marginal farmers. Economists are debating whether green revolution has aggravated inter-personal inequalities in rural areas? The studies of G.R. Saini and Pranab Bardhan indicate that large farmers have gained the most from green revolution. Contrarily, the findings of J.R. Westley and George Blyn reveal that small farmers have also benefited from green revolution and that the gap between the rich and the poor has narrowed down in the rural sector. There is yet another view, maintaining that the new technology has been *neutral* meaning thereby that the pattern of inter-personal inequalities has remained unaffected.

C. Inter-crop Imbalances: From the beginning, the HYV Programme was confined to wheat, rice and coarse cereals like *jowar*, *bajra*, and maize. Thus, the non-foodgrains crops were excluded from the purview of new agriculture strategy. As a result, the real breakthrough has been achieved in the case of cereal crops, mainly wheat and rice. There has been no corresponding research and effort for similar success in other crops, especially pulses and oilseeds. Consequently, there has been undue pressure on the prices of pulses and dependence on the import of oilseeds.

D. Fluctuating Output: Agricultural production is marked by annual fluctuations because it is still dependent to a large extent on conditions of uncertain rainfall. Agriculture in India is rightly described as *gamble in monsoon*. The crops more prone to fluctuations are oilseeds, pulses, cotton, jute and sugarcane. This has adversely affected the capacity utilisation of agro-based industries.

E. Neutrality to Scale: Another controversy is whether new agricultural technology is neutral to scale? According to agricultural scientists the return per unit of land is uniform, i.e. the technology is neutral to scale. However, this conclusion is based on certain assumptions which include controlled water supply, selected seeds, right type of fertilisers and timely use of pesticides and insecticides. Thus, if the small and marginal farmers have not gained from new technology it is because they cannot afford it. In other words, the technology as such is neutral as between big and small farms.

Some experts have challenged the *neutrality to scale* thesis of the agricultural scientists. According to him, the physical and social conditions in the village work in favour of the big landlords. Therefore, what is true under controlled laboratory conditions is not necessarily true in field conditions. He believes that scale neutrality is a myth.

E. Social Costs: New agricultural technology is responsible for various health hazards for the farm workers. It is unfortunate that many poor workers have lost their limbs or even their lives while operating sub-standard farm machinery like thrashers. There is no well-defined provision for quick and adequate compensation to victims of machine accidents. The spray of poisonous chemicals on plants is mainly done by poor workers and it proves very injurious to their health.

The green revolution has accentuated rural class differences. It has given birth to a new acquisitive society in rural areas. The result is moral degradation, social tensions, and violence. The new agricultural strategy at best is a mixed blessing.

1.8 Agricultural Price Policy, Food Subsidy and Public Distribution System

For the large sections of the community which live near the margin of subsistence, a certain minimum supply of foodgrains at reasonable prices constitutes the rock-bottom of the standard of living, a fall in which would be seriously detrimental to health and efficiency. Foodgrains occupy a pivotal place in the price structure, and if this latter has to be safeguarded, as it must be, the prices of foodgrains must be held stable at levels within the reach of the poorer sections of the community.

The objectives of a sound agricultural price policy are two-fold (a) to ensure fair prices for the produce of the farmers and (b) to ensure adequate and regular supply of agricultural commodities to the consumers at reasonable prices.

Excessive fluctuations in agricultural prices generate harmful effects both for the producers and the consumers. The beneficiaries of unstable prices are the middlemen and the speculators. It is for these reasons that Government undertakes buffer stocks operations, i.e. making purchases when there is glut of produce in the market and releasing stocks during period of scarcity.

1.8.1 Minimum Support Prices: An important element of the agricultural price policy of the Government of India is the announcement every year of minimum support prices for major commodities. The co-operative societies and government agencies have helped the farmers to escape the exploitative practices of the private traders. The Price Support Policy of the Government is directed at providing insurance to agricultural producers against any sharp fall in farm prices. The minimum guaranteed prices are fixed to set a floor below which market prices cannot fall. Trends in MSP of wheat and paddy in recent years are given in Table 1.3.

1.8.2 Food Subsidy: Producers and consumers and within this group the vulnerable sections of the society are the major beneficiaries of food subsidy. The subsidy incurred on the supply of foodgrains through the PDS at below FCI's economic cost constitutes the consumer subsidy while the producer subsidy is the direct offshoot of the price support based procurement operations of the government. The producer subsidy together with the cost of maintaining the buffer stock accounts for the cost of buffer stock operations. The consumer subsidy together with the buffer carrying cost constitutes the food subsidy.

The food subsidy bill has increased from year to year in recent times (Table 1.4). Though pruning of the existing subsidy level is imperative and could be done by reducing operational inefficiency, the interests of the poor also have to be safeguarded. The surplus stocks of foodgrains with the government provide a vital resource for providing income support to the poor and the vulnerable. Better targeting of subsidies is now beginning to be visible. But it has been found that PDS has failed in large parts of the country, and that it needs to be restructured to be an effective tool of food security.

Table 1.3: Minimum Support/Procurement Price of Wheat and Paddy in Recent Years (Rs./quintal)

Crop Year	Wheat		Paddy (Common)	
	MSP	Per cent change	MSP	Per cent change
1997-98	510	7.4	415	9.2
1998-99	550	7.8	440	6.0
1999-00	580	5.5	490	11.4
2000-01	610	5.2	510	4.1
2001-02	620	1.6	530	3.9
2002-03	620	-	530	-
2003-04	630	1.6	550	3.8
2004-05	640	1.6	560	1.8
2005-06	650	1.6	570	1.8
2006-07	750	15.4	580	1.8

Source: Government of India, *Economic Survey,* 2006-07, p. 103, Table 5.19.

Minimum support prices (MSP) lay the floor for the market price of foodgrains, especially the two dominant foodgrains: rice and wheat. With sharp increases in MSP every year despite surpluses having replaced shortages, the MSP has become the maximum selling price instead of being the floor price. This coupled with the system of open-ended procurement has made FCI the buyer of the first resort resulting in huge accumulation of surplus public stocks of foodgrains, leading to much higher commitments for government subsidy. FCI has thus become the main buyer, stockiest and seller in the domestic market. It is also the main exporter.

Table 1.4: Growth of Food Subsidies in India in Recent Years

(Rs. crore)

Year	Food subsidy	As per cent of GDP#
1999-00	9,435	0.48
2000-01	12,060	0.57
2001-02	17,499	0.77
2002-03	24,176	0.99
2003-04	25,160	0.91
2004-05	25,800	0.83
2005-06*	23,200	0.66
2006-07**	24,200	---

New series based on 1999-00.

* Revised estimates; ** Budget estimates.

Source: Government of India, *Economic Survey,* 2006-07, p. 105, Table 5.22.

1.8.3 Public Distribution System (PDS): Food Security is one of the major components of social security. It consists of ensuring that 'food is available at all times, that all persons have means of and access to it, that it is nutritionally adequate in terms of quantity, quality and variety, and that it is acceptable within the given culture'. There are three elements in this definition, availability, access and suitability. In recent years, nutrition has been considered as part of food security, and is therefore, referred to as 'Food and Nutrition Security'.

There is enough food available in the world. Even in developing countries, the per capita food production has increased by 8 per cent on an average in the 1980s. Everybody can get 2,500 calories from the available food which is 200 calorie more than the basic minimum. What is required is a well-organised public distribution system. Efforts have been made to streamline the PDS through the introduction of the Targeted Public Distribution System in June 1997. This system follows a two tier subsidised pricing structure for families Below Poverty Line (BPL) and for those Above Poverty Line. BPL population receives rice and wheat at a much lower price (hence highly subsidised) whereas APL population is supplied at a price which is much higher and closer to the economic cost. The identification of the poor under the scheme is done by the States.

Antyodaya Anna Yojana launched in December 2000 aims at identifying 10 million poor families and providing them with 25 kgs of foodgrains per family per month, at a price of Rs. 2 per kg. for wheat and Rs. 3 per kg for rice, amounting to an annual allocation of foodgrains of about 30 lakh tonnes.

Similarly, the Anna Purna Scheme (2000) is for senior citizens eligible for old age pension but not receiving the pension, and whose children are not residing with them. Under this scheme 10 kg of foodgrains is provided per person, per month, free of cost. The estimated cost of this scheme is Rs. 330 crore per annum.

Public Distribution System (PDS) is the cornerstone of Government's price policy and food security system in India. It ensures availability of certain essential commodities (sugar, kerosene, rice and wheat) at affordable prices, especially for the poor. Through its agency the Food Corporation of India (FCI), the Government procures and stocks foodgrains, which are released every month for distribution through the PDS network across the country. These commodities are distributed to the public through a network of Fair Price Shops (FPS). In addition to this, the system of procurement is also used by the Government to provide minimum support prices to the farmers in order to stabilise agricultural output and income.

The FCI issues foodgrains to the State Governments at a uniform Central Issue Price (CIP) which is considerably lower than the economic cost incurred by the Central Government by way of procurement, storage, transport and distribution. The difference between the economic cost and the CIP is called the consumer subsidy. Since the FCI maintains a large buffer stock of foodgrains, it entails a substantial carrying cost. The consumer subsidy and the carrying cost together add up to the total food subsidy which is borne by the Central Government. It is an important item of the non-Plan revenue expenditure of the Government as shown in its annual budget.

1.8.4 Targeted Public Distribution System (TPDS): A well-targeted and properly functioning Public Distribution System (PDS) is an important constituent of the strategy for poverty alleviation. PDS is operated under the joint responsibility of the Central and State Governments. The Central Government takes the responsibility for procurement, storage, transportation and bulk allocation of foodgrains, at subsidized prices. The responsibility of distribution to consumers including target groups through a network of 4,63,000 fair price shops rests with the State Governments.

TPDS was introduced in 1997 in order to achieve better targeting of food subsidy. Under the TPDS, a dual price mechanism for Above the Poverty Line (APL) and Below the Poverty Line (BPL) consumers prevails. The full economic cost of foodgrains is recovered from the APL consumers while foodgrains are sold at half the economic cost to BPL consumers.

1.9 Impact of Globalisation on Agriculture

Globalisation is widely seen as the most important factor that could influence economies of nations the world over in the new millennium. The rapid advancement in information technology and communications has made it not just possible but absolutely essential for industry the world over to adapt or fall by the wayside.

The most important aspects of economic globalisation are:

- breaking down of national barriers;

- international spread of trade, financial and production activities, and
- growing power of transnational corporations and international financial institutions in these processes.

The issue that concerns developing countries is how one can ensure greater participation of the weaker economies, particularly backward regions of these economies, in the global process and what needs to be done to ensure that the course of globalisation benefits more people in more countries.

Globalisation has profoundly affected both the ways of life and the livelihoods of indigenous people worldwide. Dr. D. Swaminathan, an Agricultural Scientist, deplores that one crore farmers in USA have been getting US$ 100 crore of subsidies per day as against 11 crore farmers in India who are desperately looking up to the skies without any substantial subsidy as in the case of their counterparts in the USA to adopt new technologies of production with the latest equipments, to buy improved seeds and pesticides to boost up their productivity levels. It is because of the fact the Government of India under the dictates of World Bank has significantly reduced the agriculture subsidies

Globalisation of agriculture mainly implies the exposure of Indian agriculture to international market forces through free exports and imports of agricultural commodities. Globalisation of Indian agriculture, on the one hand, will provide it with opportunities to share the international market and on the other, will expose it to competition form foreign suppliers in the domestic market and force the domestic production to adopt more efficient techniques of production. In general the economists hold that on the whole, India is likely to benefit form the globalisation of Indian agriculture. This is because India has a comparative cost advantage in the production of agricultural commodities. It is felt that agricultural exports form India are likely to increase significantly if the government follows policy of globalizing the Indian economy.

However, the immediate impact rise in agricultural exports

will be an increase in the prices of agricultural commodities in the national market. And if these commodities include wheat and rice or other cereals, the vulnerable section of the society will be hit hard. This will necessitate a more effective implementation of the Public Distribution System (PDS). This may also result in food subsidies. One important way is to develop and adopt cost effective technology for production of agricultural products. Reduction in cost of production will surely keep the internal prices of agricultural commodities stable even when these are exported. National Agricultural Research System (NARS) needs to be revamped to suit the changing conditions in the country. There exists a large potential for increasing exports of quite a few agricultural commodities produced in India. However, despite the great potential for increase in agricultural exports, various economists suggest caution in completely freeing exports, especially of food grains to other countries.

There is a need to regulate the exports, not only for reason of food security but also for some other politico-economic considerations. Specific steps have to be earnestly taken to generate this surplus. This implies development of infrastructure especially irrigation and power research, extension of new technology to uncovered crops and areas, development of market infrastructure and a more efficient use of existing resources. Further, in view of the increasing competition in the world market, it will also be necessary to pay special attention to the improvement in the quality of the products to be exported. Import of agricultural commodities unrelated to the scarcity of these commodities in the country will only mean a wasteful use of foreign exchange. Another reason for overseeing the imports of agricultural commodities is the need to ensure that the imported agricultural commodities are not hoarded for profiteering by the private individuals.

Besides development of infrastructure, multinationals can be allowed to develop agro-processing industries. But we have to be cautions while recommending such a step for some other productive activities allied to agriculture. In this connection, we must refer to the consequences of having allowed them the right of fishing in the Indians seas. A large number of Indian fisherman has been rendered unemployed because of the grant of these rights to multinationals. However, the provisions of the TRIPS are likely to attract the development of agriculture rather adversely at least for some time. This provision implies the technologies used in the production of to traded goods will be patented and their use for production will not be made by any country except the one where it has been patented. So far as agriculture is concerned, it is the cost of new varieties of imported seeds which will increase as the technology used in their development is obviously a foreign one. In order to overcome this problem, we have set up our own research projects to develop new seeds with indigenous technology.

1.10 Relief Package for Distress Prone Districts

Moved by a large number of suicides by farmers in certain parts of the country, Government of India identified 31 districts in four states, viz., Andhra Pradesh (16), Maharashtra (6), Karnataka (6) and Kerala (3) where the incidence of farmers' suicides has been very high and launched a special rehabilitation package to mitigate their distress. The package, inter alia, envisaged waiving of interest on overdue loans, as on 1 July 2006, and making them eligible for fresh loan and rescheduling of overdue loan over a period of 3 to 5 years. An amount of Rs. 2,718 crore is expected to be waived in these districts and will be shared equally between the Union Government and the concerned State Government. During 2006-07, institutional credit flow of Rs. 21, 422 crore was to be ensured in these 31 districts. In the Union Budget 2007-08, a Special Plan relating to farm credit, involving a sum of Rs. 16,979 crore, including Rs. 12,400 crore for water related schemes, has been announced. The Plan includes a provision of Rs.153 crore for induction of high yielding milch animals and related activities to augment income of farmers.

1.11 Farmers' Suicide in India

Of the 1.5 lakh Indian farmers who took their own lives between 1997 and 2005, nearly two-thirds did so in the States of Maharashtra, Andhra Pradesh, Karnataka, and Madhya Pradesh (including Chhattisgarh). The number of Indians committing suicide each year rose from around 96,000 in 1997 to roughly 1.14 lakh in 2005. In the same period, the number of farmers taking their own lives each year shot up dramatically, from under 14,000 in 1997 to over 17,000 in 2005. While the rise in farm suicides has been on for over a decade, there have been sharp spurts in some years. For instance, 2004 saw well over 18,200 farm suicides across India. Almost two-third of these was in the Big Four or 'Suicide SEZ' States. The year 1998, too, saw a huge increase over the previous year. Farm suicides crossed the 16,000 mark, beating the preceding year by nearly 2,400 such deaths. Farm suicides as a proportion of total suicides rose from 14.2 in 1997 to 15.0 in 2005. The ACGR for all suicides in India over a nine-year period is 2.18 per cent. This is not very much higher than the population growth rate. But for farm suicides it is much higher, at nearly 3 (or 2.91) per cent.

On average, one Indian farmer committed suicide every 32 minutes between 1997 and 2005. Since 2002, that has become one suicide every 30 minutes. On an average, one farmer took his or her life every 53 minutes between 1997 and 2005 in just the States of Maharashtra, Andhra Pradesh, Karnataka and Madhya Pradesh (including Chhattisgarh). In Maharashtra alone, there was one suicide every three hours. It got even worse after 2001. It rose to one farm suicide every 48 minutes in these Big Four States and one every two and quarter hours in Maharashtra alone. The Big Four have together seen 89,362 farmers' suicides between 1997 and 2005, or 44,102 between 2002 and 2005.

Farmers, suicides as a percentage of total farmers are hard to calculate on a yearly basis. A clear national 'farm suicide rate' can be derived only for 2001. That is because we have the

Census to tell us how many farmers there were in the country that year. For other years, the figure would be a conjecture, however plausible. But even in 2001, when the farm suicides were not yet at their worst, the farm suicide rate (FSR) at 12.9 was much higher than the general suicide rate (GSR) at 10.6 for that year. But the GSR slowed down after that to 10.3 by 2005 even as the total number of suicides went up. It means that the increase in the number of general suicides did not keep pace with the growth in general population. But the FSR seems to have risen more steeply after 2001. By all accounts, while the number of farm suicides kept increasing, the number of farmers has fallen since 2001, with countless thousands abandoning agriculture.

In 2005, the Big Four or 'Suicide SEZ' States accounted for 43.9 per cent of all suicides and 64.0 per cent of all farm suicides in the country. By contrast, a group of States with the highest general suicide rates – including Tamil Nadu, Kerala, West Bengal, Tripura, and Pondicherry – accounted for 20.5 per cent of farm suicides in India. "Their share of both total suicides and of farmers' suicides declined between 1997 and 2005 even as that of the Big Four steadily rose," points out Professor K. Nagaraj of the Madras Institute of Development Studies (MIDS).

Unfortunately due to uncertain monsoon, non-availability of credit, increasing prices of seeds, pesticides and fertilizers, agriculture has become a most critical industry and farmers are suffering due to economic distress and they are committing suicide on large scale in different provinces. The expenditure on sowing, cropping and final yield becomes more than the production itself or many a times farmer has to incur loans for marriages, festivals or rituals, which he cannot meet out on the basis of limited production, which is again uncertain. In this critical situation, he goes in psychological depression and commits suicide, when he feels that there is no way out for the future. "Unfortunately this egalitarian idea has not been successful and Indian farmers in spite of competing in the global market are trailing behind and they are fighting for their existence." The reasons for farmers committing suicide are examined in the following manner.

During last few decades agricultural production process has become difficult due to increased expenditure. The cost of seeds, fertilizer, organic farming techniques, new harvesting equipments, tractors, increase in the cost of manual labor etc. are major factors for increased expenditure on production. Farmers feel that it is better to sell agricultural land than to suffer in its vicious circle. For these purpose if he draws loan and if he is not able to repay it, he again enrolls himself for fresh loan, which he cannot meet and the vicious circle goes on increasing.

Indian farmers produce different types of product, such as Jawar, wheat, rice, sugarcane, cotton and vegetables and fruits as well. However, there is no proper education and orientation for the search of new markets. The brokers at district level exploit farmers and large stake of the profit goes to these brokers and farmers remain neglected. Lack of fixed price and lack of nearby markets are the two reasons responsible for exploitation of farmers. The farmers have to meet out their day to day responsibilities in a systematic manner. Unfortunately in village area the farmers are more predominantly superstitious and religious. They follow customs and traditions and they prefer to celebrate marriages during early age of their wards to overcome their responsibility.

The farmer when he is in a good season receives better profits, than his earlier phase and in good moods he makes more expenditure on entertainment. He attends folk festival or he becomes a drug addict, which gives him a temporary happiness. In long term the extravagance of farmers creates more complications. This extravagance affects his agricultural investment potentials and on the other side he tries to evade responsibility of debt clearance and the pending monthly installment against loans, which increases his interest on debt. The farmers when they feel it difficult to receive loans from cooperative credit system, due to their hazards and complications, turn towards indigenous bankers and suffer a great deal due to heavy burden of compound interest and transfer their land holdings on papers as credit and if they do not pay the loan in time they have to lose their land. It has been observed that in spite of different types of rules the Government has failed to control the indigenous banking system.

The farmers many a times are victims of continuous illness due to chronic diseases. In India, the health services are not available at village level and farmers have to shift from villages to metro cities for better treatment. They require heavy amount for recovery from their illness. When they do not meet these expenses based on their agro profits, there is no way than to commit suicide. Further, farmers after the WTO pact and globalization have started to suffer more because foreign fruits, food grains and even milk are available in the Indian market, which is affecting farmers' interests. However, in India due to lack of public distribution system, the stored food grains are not property distributed and malnutrition of children goes on increasing in the isolated areas.

Farm suicides in Maharashtra increased dramatically in 2006, more than in any other part of the country. The State saw 4,453 farmers' suicides that year, over a quarter of the all-India total of 17,060, according to the National Crime Records Bureau (NCRB) in its Report, Accidental Deaths and Suicides in India, 2006. The previous worst, 4,417 in 2004, was also in Maharashtra. It has seen 36,428 farmer's suicides since 1995, as per the official count. The suicides in Maharashtra mark a rise of 527 over the 2005 figure. This was four and a half times bigger than that in Andhra Pradesh, the next worst-hit State, which saw a rise of 117 farm suicides over 2005. This is also more than twice the increase of 198 in Madya Pradesh and Chhattisgarh taken together. Maharashtra's upward spike occurred in the year when the relief package of both the Prime Minister and Chief Minister, worth Rs. 4,825 crore in all, was being implemented in the Vidharbha region, where suicides have been most intense.

The NCRB figures shows an unrelenting uptrend in what can be termed the 'SEZ' or (farmers) 'Special Elimination Zone' States. These States, which account for nearly two-thirds of all farm suicides in the country, include Maharashtra, Andhra Pradesh, Karnataka and Madhya Pradesh (including Chhattisgarh). As a group, the 'SEZ' State saw an increase of 6.2 per cent in such deaths. Among them, Maharashtra - 4,453, Andhra Pradesh - 2,607 and Madhya Pradesh-Chhattisgarh - 2,858 show a sharp upward spike. Karnataka – 1720, reports a decline. So though the all India numbers for 2006 reflect a very small decline of 61 over the 2005 figure of 17,131, the broad trends of the last decade continue and the trend of rapidly rising farm suicides, particularly post-2001 in the 'SEZ' States, remains unchanged.

Hence, the minuscule decline in the figure for the country as a whole marks no break from the dismal decade-long trend. NCRB data recorded 1,66,304 farmers' suicides in a decade since 1997. Of these, 78,737 occurred between 1997 and 2001. The next five years-from 2002 to 2006 proved worse, seeing 87,567 farmers take their own lives.

This reflects that on average, there has been one farmer's suicide every 30 minutes since 2002. Prime Minister Manmohan Singh on February 8, 2008 said that the Government would soon come out with loan relief measures for farmers, since in many parts of the country the farmers are suffering under the burden of mounting loans and it will lead them to committing suicides further.

1.12 Post-1991 Initiatives in Indian Agriculture

Economic reforms initiated in 1991 have largely bypassed the agricultural sector. A few initial steps have been taken but they are by no means adequate. Agricultural growth decelerated during the 1990s. Per capita foodgrain availability has remained below the historic peak attained in 1991.

Agricultural performance witnessed a dip in the 1990s partly on account of subdued public investment in agriculture and inadequate diversification. The decline in public investment was only partially compensated by the rise in private investment. Agricultural sector in the 1990s witnessed slowdown but at the same time recorded unprecedented accumulation of footstock due to persistent price distortions through MSP. The impulses of reforms have been relatively less in scope and depth in the agricultural sector. Nevertheless, a series of policy initiatives have been undertaken in this sector as well.

1.12.1 National Agriculture Policy, 2000: On July 28, 2000, Government of India announced a National Agriculture Policy to include this vital sector of the economy in the ambit of economic reforms. According to *Economic Survey,* 2000-2001, "After the economic reforms in 1991-92 that removed the restrictive and protective licensing regime for industry, the policy focus turned to agriculture. There is still the general impression that agriculture in India operates amidst a number of restraints and controls and that farmers do not receive the benefits of free trade as compared to other sectors of the economy." [6] The main elements of the new agriculture policy are the following.

- Private sector investment in agriculture would be encouraged, particularly in areas like agricultural research, human resource development, post harvest management and marketing.
- Catapulting agricultural growth to over 4 per cent per annum by 2005.
- Restrictions on the movement of agricultural commodities throughout the country would be progressively dismantled.
- Appropriate measures would be adopted to ensure that agriculturists by and large, remain outside the regulatory and tax collection system.
- Rural electrification would be given high priority as a prime mover for agricultural development.

- Progressive institutionalisation of rural and farm credit would be continued for providing timely and adequate credit to farmers.

1.12.2 Development of Food Processing Industry: The shelf life of foodgrains is over 3 years or even more as against fruits and vegetables whose shelf life ranges between 1 week and 3 months. Currently hardly 1 per cent of over 140 million tonnes of fruits and vegetables produces in the country goes through the processing route. Hence strategies for diversified agriculture should involve a separate road map for value addition in fruits and vegetables sector. Creation of essential infrastructure for preservation, cold storage, refrigerated transportation, rapid transit, grading, processing, packaging and quality control would be the key areas for such a strategy.

The Ministry of Food Processing is setting up food parks in different parts of the country. The idea behind setting up of food parks is to enable small and medium entrepreneurs find access to capital-intensive facilities, such as cold storage, warehouse, quality control labs, effluent treatment plants etc. Development of such facilities is expected to make the food processing units in the food parks cost competitive besides improving their market accessibility. So far 30 food parks have been sanctioned in different parts of the country. The Ministry is also in the process of introducing a new Plan Scheme for development of infrastructure like cold storage etc. for the benefit of food processing units in addition to the scheme of food parks already in existence.

The Ministry is also operating Plan schemes on the promotion of total quality management including ISO 9000, ISO 14000, Hazard Analysis and Critical Control Points (HACCP), good manufacturing practices, good hygienic practices etc. with the following objectives.

- To motivate the food processing industries for adoption of food safety and quality assurance mechanism.
- To prepare them to face the global competition in the international trades in the post WTO era.

- To enable adherence to a stringent quality in hygiene norms.
- To enhance product acceptance by overseas buyers.
- To keep Indian Food Industry technologically abreast of international best practices.

In addition, Ministry of Food Processing is also working towards the promotion of bar coding on food packages, as the bar coding is on its way to become almost a compulsory requirement in the global market.

1.12.3 ***Vishesh Krishi Upaj Yojana:*** The objective of the scheme is to promote export of fruits, vegetables, flowers, minor forest produce, and their value added products, by incentivising exporters of such products.

A. Entitlement: Exporters of such products shall be entitled for duty credit scrip equivalent to 5 per cent of the FOB value of exports for each licencing year commencing from April 1, 2004. The scrip and the items imported against it would be freely transferable.

B. Imports Allowed: Duty credit may be used for import of inputs or goods including capital goods, as may be notified, provided the same is freely importable under ITC (HS). Imports from a port other than the port of export shall be allowed under TRA (Telegraphic Release Advice) facility as per the terms and conditions of the notification issued by Department of Revenue.

C. Cenvat/Drawback: Additional customs duty/excise duty paid in cash or through debit under Vishesh Krishi Upaj Yojana shall be adjusted as CENVAT Credit or Duty Drawback as per rules framed by the Department of Revenue.

1.12.4 Crop Diversification Measures: India's future agricultural development will require much faster crop diversification in view of changes in consumption pattern. There is growing preference for milk and milk products, meat, poultry, fish, fruits and vegetables. Areas like horticulture and floriculture also hold promise as they have higher export potential.

According to RBI, "A contributing factor to below-potential performance of agriculture is the failure to sufficiently diversify the cropping pattern. The minimum support price (MSP) policy has distorted the relative prices between rice and wheat, on the one hand, and other food and non-food crops, on the other., giving rise to a distorted cropping pattern. It has contributed to a steep rise in the ratio of procurement to production over the years. The higher increase in MPPs of rice and wheat relative to prices of other agricultural commodities has contributed to an incentive structure that favours production of rice and wheat at the cost of other crops. The policy has contributed to a burgeoning stock – far in excess of food security requirements, adding to carrying costs and locked-in bank credit, which could have been otherwise deployed for funding productive activities." [7]

1.12.5 Emphasis on Horticultural Crops: The Government has identified horticultural crops as a means of diversification for making agriculture more profitable through efficient land use, optimum utilization of natural resources (soil, water and environment) and creating skilled employment for rural masses, especially women folk. Recent efforts have been rewarding in terms of increased production and productivity and availability of a much larger volume of horticultural produce. India has emerged as the largest producer of coconut, arecanut, cashewnut, ginger, turmeric, black pepper and the second largest producer of fruits and vegetables. Among the new crops, kiwi, olive crops and oil palm have been successfully introduced for commercial cultivation in the country. Some improvement is seen in the adoption of technology for raising production.

Efforts are on to encourage private investment in hi-tech horticulture with micro-propagation, protected cultivation, drip irrigation, and integrated nutrient and pest management besides making use of latest post-harvest technology particularly in the case of perishable commodities. As a result, horticulture crop production has begun to move from rural confines to commercial ventures and has attracted young entrepreneurs, since it has proved to be intellectually satisfying and economically rewarding.

A large variety of fruits are grown in India. Of these, mango, banana, citrus, pineapple, papaya, guava, sapota, jackfruit, litchi and grapes are some of the tropical and sub-tropical fruits and nuts. Apple, pear, peach, plum, apricot, almond and walnut constitute the temperate fruits and nuts. Aonia, ber, pomegranate, annona, fig and phalsa are some of the arid zone fruits. India produces over 46 million tonnes of fruits accounting for about 10 per cent of the world production. The country ranks first in the production of mango, banana, sapota and acid lime and, in recent years recorded the highest productivity in grape.

Mango is the most important fruit covering about 39 per cent of the area accounting for 23 per cent of total fruit production in the country. India's share in the world production of mango is about 54 per cent. Citrus ranks second in area and accounts for about 10 per cent of country's fruit production. Limes, lemons, sweet orange and mandarin cover bulk of the area under this group of fruits. Banana ranks third in area covering about 13 per cent of the total area. It ranks first in fruit production contributing nearly one-third of total fruit production. Apple is the fourth major fruit crop of the country with production of 1.42 million tonnes. The share of other fruits like guava and papaya is about 4 per cent while that of grapes and pineapple is about 2 percent and litchi, about 1 per cent. The arid zones of the country are potential areas for fruits like aonia, ber, pomegranate, annona, etc. There has been a steady increase in the area and production of these fruits particularly aonia, ber and pomegranate in the country as a result of identification and development of suitable varieties and production technologies. In addition to these, date palm and fig cultivation is also finding favour in some areas.

Vegetables constitute the most important food next only to cereals and milk. Important vegetable crops grown in the country include potato, tomato, onion, brinjal, cabbage, cauliflower, okra and peas. India occupies first position in the production of cauliflower, second in onion and third in cabbage production in the world.

Traditional flowers such as jasmine, marigold, chrysanthemum, tuberose, crossandra and aster are commonly grown. Commercial cultivation of cut flowers such as rose, orchids, gladiolus, carnation, anthurium, gerbera and lilies has also become popular. The total production of flowers during 2001-02 was 0.57 million tonnes of loose flowers and 803.5 million numbers of cut flowers. Although flower cultivation has been practised in India since time immemorial, floriculture has blossomed into a viable business only in recent years. Considering the potential of this sector for generation of income and employment opportunities, promotion of involvement of women and enhancement of exports, it has been identified as an Extreme Focus Area for exports by the Government.

1.12.6 Measures to Boost Plantation Sector: The Government of India has taken a series of steps to promote tea, coffee and rubber plantations.

A. Tea

- Replacement of the central excise duty payable on tea by an additional duty of excise of Re. 1 per Kg for creating a separate fund for long term development and modernisation of the tea plantation sector.
- Increasing the allowance under Section 33 AB of the Income Tax Act from 20 per cent to 40 per cent.
- Implementation of a credit relief package announced by RBI and IBA to help the tea industry.
- Introduction of a price sharing formula for equitable sharing of the sale proceeds between the Bought Leaf Factories and small tea growers.
- Implementation of IT based Information Dissemination Plan for the tea industry, including conversion of manual auction centers into electronic auction centers.

B. Coffee

- Re-phasement/restructuring of loans taken by the coffee growers from commercial banks.
- Providing interest relief to coffee growers on their working capital loans taken from financial institutions.
- Undertaking campaigns to promote domestic consumption of coffee.
- Reduction of import duty on specified machinery for coffee sector to 5 per cent to enable the industry to improve the quality and productivity of coffee for making it globally competitive.
- Convincing the Commercial Banks to provide working capital loans to coffee growers at reduced interest rates.

C. Rubber

- A number of plan schemes are being implemented. These schemes provide for suitable financial/technical assistance to the growers, processors, exporters etc for increasing production of natural rubber through expansion of area, enhancing productivity, improving the quality of produce to achieve competitiveness in the global markets and promoting agricultural and technological research in the interest of the industry.
- In the context of boosting export of natural rubber and establishing India as regular exporter of this commodity, Government is implementing an Export Promotion of Natural Rubber Scheme since 2001-02. The scheme inter-alia provides for financial assistance to the exporters of NR for quality upgradation, certification, transportation etc.
- To regulate the import of inferior rubber coming into the country, which was passing as standard rubber, Government has enforced conformity with BIS standards on imported rubber also, as in the case of domestic rubber.
- Implementation of a Price Stabilization Fund Scheme with a corpus of Rs. 500 crore for the benefit of the growers of tea, coffee, rubber and tobacco.

1.12.7 Marine Fishing Policy, 2004: Fisheries sector occupies a very important place in the socio-economic development of the country. It has been recognised as a powerful income and employment generator as it stimulates growth of a number of subsidiary industries and is a source of cheap and nutritious food besides being a foreign exchange earner. At the same time it is an instrument of livelihood for a large section of economically backward population of the country.

A. Policy Objectives: Policy objectives of the Marine Fishing Policy, 2004 are the following.

- To augment marine fish production of the country up to the sustainable level in a responsible manner so as to boost export of sea food from the country and also to increase per capita fish protein intake of the masses.
- To ensure socio-economic security of the artisan fishermen whose livelihood solely depends on this vocation.
- To ensure sustainable development of marine fisheries with due concern for ecological integrity and bio-diversity.

B. Main Provisions of the Policy: These are as follows.

- **Marine Fisheries Resources:** The policy underscores the need for a departure from the open access concept in the territorial waters besides putting in place stringent management regimes. Promoting exploitation in the deep sea and oceanic waters would be another approach for reducing fishing pressure in the traditional fishing areas.
- **Harvesting of Marine Fish Resources:** The policy advocates protection, consideration and encouragement of subsistence level fishermen and technology transfer to small scale sector and infrastructure support to industrial sector. There would be exclusive areas in terms of depth and (or) distance earmarked for non-mechanised (non-motorised) traditional craft. An area beyond this would be demarcated for mechanized and motorised craft.
- **Post-harvest Operations:** Total utilisation of harvested fish for food and non-food uses would be the central

theme. Efforts would be made to fully comply with international requirements in post harvest care of catch so as to achieve highest standards in food safety. It would also be the concern of the Government to ensure that the post-harvest losses are minimized.

- **Resource Management:** Exploitation of living resources within 50 metres depth zone is showing symptoms of depletion and in certain belts in the onshore waters, it tends to cross optimum sustainable levels. The policy therefore advocates a stringent fishery management system to be in place.
- **Fishermen Welfare:** Fishing is the sole livelihood for about 10 lakh fishermen households along the coastline and this policy attaches top priority to ensuring their social security and economic well being.
- **Environmental Aspects:** The effect of environmental factors on the health of living resources needs increased attention in tune with the international awareness on the issue. Health hazards due to consumption of fish harvested from contaminated water is also becoming a matter of great concern in many parts of the world. The agencies responsible for legislation relating to environmental pollution would be urged to implement them more stringently so that the impact of pollution on fisheries can be minimized.
- **Infrastructure Development for Marine Fisheries:** Development of infrastructure for marine fisheries is of vital importance and should have an integrated approach. The facilities would inter alia include jetties, landing centres, provision for fuel, water, ice, repairs to vessels and gear. The concept of hygienic post harvest handling of fish would also be woven into the project.
- **Legislative Support:** An enabling legal framework is an essential pre-requisite for proper management and control of fisheries sector. As at present, the subject of fisheries is in the State list under article 21 of the Indian Constitution,

management and control of coastal fisheries is vested with the maritime States and union territories. At the same time the Union Government carries out management and control of the fishing activities beyond territorial limits in the EEZ.

- **Policy for Development of Fisheries in the Union Territories of Lakshadweep and Andaman & Nicobar Islands:** The waters around these two Island Groups are rich in fish resource, which are currently exploited far below the exploitable limits. Fisheries, capture, post harvest operations and marketing, is still an important means of livelihood for the inhabitants of these islands. It is, therefore considered relevant to have the policy initiatives in respect of the two UTs.

1.12.8 National Commission on Farmers: National Commission on Farmers (Chairman: M.S. Swaminathan) was set up in 2004 to suggest an action plan for farmers and farm sector. The Commission submitted five Reports between December 2005 and October, 2006. Main recommendations of the Commission are incorporated in the Revised Draft National Policy for Farmers. These include the following.

- Asset reforms covering land, water, livestock and bio-resources.
- Farmer-friendly support services covering extension, training and knowledge, connectivity, credit and insurance.
- Assured and remunerative marketing.
- Inputs and delivery services.
- Curriculum reforms in the agriculture universities.
- Bringing Agriculture in the Concurrent List of the Constitution.
- Setting up of a National Food Security and Sovereignty Board.
- Universalization of PDS.
- Setting up of an Indian Trade Organization.
- Making the Commission on Agriculture Cost and Prices into an autonomous statutory organization with MSP at

least 50 per cent more than the cost of production.

- Launch of a Rural Non-farm Livelihood Initiative (RNFLI).

1.12.9 Eleventh Five Year Plan (2007-12) on Agriculture: Expressing concern on agricultural crisis and outlining strategy to regain agricultural dynamism, the Approach Paper on Eleventh Five Year Plan released by the Government in November 2006 observed, "One of the major challenges of the 11th Plan will be to reverse the deceleration in agricultural growth from 3.2% observed between 1980 and 1996-97 to a trend average of around 2.0% subsequently. This deceleration is the root cause of the problem of rural distress that has surfaced in many parts of the country and reached crisis levels in some. Low farm incomes due to inadequate productivity growth have often combined with low prices of output and with lack of credit at reasonable rates to push many farmers into crippling debt. Even otherwise, uncertainties seem to have increased (regarding prices, quality of inputs and also weather and pests) which, coupled with unavailability of proper extension and risk insurance have led farmers to despair. This has also led to widespread distress migration, a rise in the number of female headed households in rural areas and a general increase in women's work burden and vulnerability. In 2004-05, women accounted for 34% of principal and 89% of subsidiary workers in agriculture, higher than in any previous round of the National Sample Survey.

The crisis of agriculture is not a purely distributional one arising out of the special problems of small and marginal farmers and landless labour. In fact, agricultural deceleration is affecting farms of all sizes. To reverse this trend, corrective policies must not only focus on the small and marginal farmers who continue to deserve special attention, but also on middle and large farmers who suffer from productivity stagnation arising from a variety of constraints.

It is vital to increase agricultural incomes as this sector still employs nearly 60% of our labour force. A measure of self-sufficiency is also critical for ensuring food security. A second green revolution is urgently needed to raise the growth rate of agricultural GDP to around 4%. This is not an easy task since actual growth of agricultural GDP, including forestry and fishing, is likely to be below 2% for the 10th Plan period. The challenge posed, therefore, is to at least double the rate of agricultural growth and to do so recognising demographic realities, particularly the increasing role of women." [8]

Outlining its strategy to raise agricultural output, the Plan document stated, The 11th Plan strategy to raise agricultural output will be based on the following elements:

- Double the rate of growth of irrigated area;
- Improve water management, rain water harvesting and watershed development;
- Reclaim degraded land and focus on soil quality;
- Bridge the knowledge gap through effective extension;
- Diversify into high value outputs, fruits, vegetables, flowers, herbs and spices, medicinal plants, bamboo, bio-diesel etc., but with adequate measures to ensure food security;
- Promote animal husbandry and fishery;
- Provide easy access to credit at affordable rates;
- Improve the incentive structure and functioning of markets;
- Refocus on land reforms issues. [9]

1.13 Indian Agriculture and WTO

The crisis in the agricultural sector is an outcome of the new economic policy and multilateral agreement like World Trade Organization (WTO). In the post reforms period, it has been opened up and allowed for private participation. Over the last few decades, a number of multilateral and trans-national companies which entered Indian agricultural sector, resulted in privatization and corporatization of agriculture. This pushed the mechanization of agriculture and left a great many wage earners unemployed. The commercialization of agriculture and unwise changes in the crop pattern mostly influenced by propaganda, have thrown peasants to the mercy of market. Liberalization has forced small farmers to compete in a global market where commodity prices have plummeted while the reduction of the government subsidies has made farming more expensive.

In recent years, it has been observed that the agricultural input costs have multiplied manifold. Neither has the cost of agricultural prices gone up substantially nor have farmers been compensated adequately through direct subsidy. This trend has affected most the small and marginal farmers. Modern agricultural practices require heavy investment in seeds, fertilizers, pesticides, electricity, water and mechanical support requires heavy investment. Lack of adequate long term institutional credit at low interest rates is forcing farmers to depend upon moneylenders, leading to the vicious circle of debts. In such a situation crop failures have forced farmers commit suicide.

1.13.1 Agreement of Agriculture (AoA): AoA of WTO recognises free and market-oriented trading system in agriculture. It has the following main features.

- **Tariffication:** It means conversion of all non-tariff barriers on trade such as import quota into tariffs. Tariff bindings are to be reduced under this agreement. (A tariff binding is a commitment not to exceed a particular level of tariff). Developed countries were to reduce their tariff bindings over a period of six years (1995-2000). Developing countries are to reduce their bindings over a period of ten years (1995-2004). Least developed countries are exempted from tariff reductions.
- **Market Access:** Where tariff bindings are too high, current market access has to be maintained as the amount of exports to other countries at preferential tariff rates. However, market access provisions do not apply when the commodity in question is a traditional staple in the diet of a developing country.

- **Domestic Support:** WTO member countries are subject to following obligations on domestic support to their agriculture.

1.13.2 Aggregate Measure of Support (AMS): It is the annual level of support in monetary terms extended to agricultural sector. It is the non-exempted support of the following two types: (a) product-specific support, i.e. market price support/subsidy given to the producer of a specific crop. (b) non-product specific support, i.e. total of subsidies on inputs like power, irrigation, fertilizers and credit. The AMS is calculated for each product receiving market support and is based on the price prevailing in the base period (1986-88). If AMS exceeds 5 per cent of the total value of agricultural production in the case of developed countries (10 percent for developing countries), these are to be reduced by 20 per cent over six years from 1995 (13.3 per cent over ten years for developing countries). The AMS to Indian agriculture is still below 10 per cent in terms of WTO stipulations.

However, there are many issues under the AoA which are considered against the interests of developing countries like India.

Firstly, the minimum access for import of primary goods flouts the basic rule of promoting free trade under WTO agreement. The *blue box* and *green box* subsidies are exempted from reduction commitments, leading to distortion in trade. This has been emphasized by developing countries like India which have a majority of low cost agricultural producers.

Secondly, distortions emerge from inequity in domestic subsidy discipline due to different base positions. The developed countries are heavily subsidized countries and are allowed to retain up to 80 per cent of their subsidies but developing countries can subsidise their farmers not more than 10 per cent of the total value of agricultural production. Hence, the domestic support by developed countries needs to be reduced substantially in absolute terms.

Thirdly, the domestic support measures relaxed for the

purpose of food security and PDS are allowed only in relation to the international market price and to the targeted population. However, this creates problem for countries like India with high percentage of poor population and heavy dependency on agriculture. Food security which is interlinked with the livelihood security is extremely important for densely populated countries with a large agrarian economy. These countries need enough flexibility under the AoA to take care of their food security, rural employment and livelihood concerns.

Fourthly, India has argued that for low income countries, market access and domestic support discipline should be such that their food requirements are met from domestic sources. The volatile international market can get transmitted to the domestic economy and can affect the prices of foodgrains and food entitlement of the poor. Hence, it was suggested that for development of agriculture in developing countries, diversification of *green box* subsidies should be encouraged and input subsidies allowed to crops where productivity levels are below the world average. Also, the negative product-specific support may be permitted so as to be adjusted against non-product-specific support.

Fifthly, developing countries face highest tariff rates which include the major agricultural staple foods, cereals, meat, sugar, milk, butter, cheese as well as tobacco products and cotton. A study conducted by WTO with United Nations Conference on Trade and Development (UNCTAD) suggests that tariff wedge will continue to be significantly high on account of tariff escalation which is a major factor preventing developing countries from diversifying and increasing their share of processed agricultural exports.

The Indian proposals have, by and large, been well received and endorsed by most of the developing countries as well as some of the developed countries. However, it is important that steps are taken to reap benefits of a liberalized trade regime through increased efficiency in agriculture and combat restrictions by developed countries arising from sanitary and phtyo-sanitary measures. Efficiency would be greatly enhanced with increased investment and land reforms. Also, diversification of agricultural production into agro-foods, horticulture and floriculture products and farm products with international quality standards could help to increase exports from this sector.

1.13.3 Green Box Support: It is given on items which have minimal impact on trade, e.g. pest and disease control, market intelligence, infrastructure services, relief from natural disaster, and buffer stock operations. It is an exempted support.

1.13.4 Blue Box Support: It is product-limiting subsidy and pertains mainly to the developed countries. It is exempted from reduction commitment under WTO. The developed countries subsidise their agriculture mainly under green and blue boxes.

1.13.5 Special and Differential Treatment Box Support: It includes investment subsidy to agricultural sector for farm development work like land levelling, shallow wells etc. It also includes agricultural input services to low-income and resource poor farmers. This support is mainly related to the developing countries and is exempted from reduction commitment under WTO.

1.13.6 Export Competition: WTO member countries are obliged to reduction commitments of their direct export subsidies. Developed countries are to reduce the volume of subsidised agricultural exports by 21 percent and the value of subsidies by 36 percent of the average base period 1986-88 within six years. Developing countries are to reduce the same by 14 per cent and 24 per cent respectively within ten years.

In the context of fears expressed in some quarters that liberalisation of imports would lead to surge of agricultural imports affecting Indian farmers adversely, the Economic Survey, 2001-02 observed, "India has considerable flexibility to counter flooding of the Indian market by cheap agriculture imports by imposing tariffs (bound rate) under WTO for agriculture products which provide a fair level of protection.

The Government, in fact, raised the import tariff for many agriculture products such as tea, coffee, pulses and edible oils in the last budget (2001-02). Countervailing duties can also be imposed to counter actionable subsidies given to agriculture products by the exporting countries apart from having the option of acting under safeguard provisions to counter surge of imports." [10]

1.13.7 Agriculture at Hong Kong Ministerial Conference of WTO, December 2005: India is a founder member of WTO. It has taken active interest in the deliberations of WTO. In fact, India has emerged as the leading voice of the developing world at various rounds of trade negotiations.

At the Doha round of trade negotiations, Members adopted a Framework Agreement outlining the elements and principles which would guide further negotiations. The framework, detailed modalities and specific commitments of each Member in respect of Agriculture and Non-Agricultural Market Access (NAMA) were discussed at the Sixth Ministerial Conference of WTO held at Hong Kong, China in December 2005.

Negotiations on agriculture, which have been taking place in special sessions of the WTO Committee on Agriculture, focused on achieving progressive and substantial reforms in global agricultural trade. While the discussions leading to Cancun had centered around bridging the divergence between the common positions taken by the European Community (EC) and US and those of the G-20 alliance, post-Cancun deliberations strengthened the G-20 alliance and emphasized their outreach to others, in particular, the G-33 alliance of developing countries on Special Products, the Africa Group, and the Cairns Group of agricultural exporting countries. The G-20 was successful in exposing the EC-US as demandeurs of substantial market access in developing countries, in particular, the large and relatively more advanced among them, and without regard to their legitimate food and livelihood security and rural development concerns, with only minimal market access commitments being called forth from themselves.

The G-20 also emphasized the requirement to eliminate all forms of export subsidies within a credible timeframe and to achieve substantial reductions in trade-distorting domestic support. In the lead up to the WTO General Council Decision of August 1, 2004 (Framework Agreement), the negotiations among the Five Interested Parties (FIPs), comprising of EC, US, Australia, Brazil and India, resolved the divergent positions on key aspects of each of the three pillars in the agriculture negotiations.

The Framework Agreement explicitly agrees to eliminate export subsidies by a credible end date. It imposes a down payment of 20 per cent on overall trade-distorting domestic support in the first year of implementation, besides containing a combination of cuts, disciplines and monitoring requirements in the various elements of the domestic support pillar, and a tiered formula for tariff reductions based on proportionately lower commitments by developing countries than by developed countries. The Framework also recognizes the critical importance of agriculture to the economic development of developing countries and the need to enable them to pursue agricultural policies that are supportive of their development goals, poverty reduction strategies, food security and livelihood concerns, including through instruments such as Special Products and a new Special Safeguard Mechanism against likely import surges. The Framework, thus, provides a useful basis for further negotiations on detailed modalities that could help create market access opportunities for products of export interest and safeguard small and vulnerable producers of farm products.

The Ministerial Declaration adopted at the end of the conference called for conclusion of negotiations launched at Doha, and established time-frames and targets in specific areas

- Resolve to complete the Doha Work Programme fully, and to conclude negotiations in 2006.

- To establish modalities in agriculture and nonagricultural market access (NAMA) by April 30, 2006 and prepare draft Schedules by July 31, 2006.
- To eliminate export subsidies in agriculture by 2013, with a substantial part in the first half of the implementation period. Developing countries without Aggregate Measurement of Support (AMS), such as India, will be exempt from reductions in *de minimis* and the overall cut in trade-distorting domestic support, consisting of AMS, the Blue Box and *de minimis*, that is entitlement to provide Amber Box subsidies up to 10 per cent of value.
- To submit a second round of revised services' offers by July 31, 2006 and submit final draft schedules by October 31, 2006.
- Amendment to TRIPS Agreement reaffirmed to address public health concerns of developing countries.
- Duty-free, quota-free market access for all LDCs' products to all developed countries. Developing country declaring itself to be in a position to do so, to also provide such access, though flexibility in coverage and in the phase in of their commitments is provided.
- In cotton, export subsidies to be eliminated by developed countries in 2006 and trade-distorting domestic subsidies to be reduced more ambitiously and over a shorter period of time.

1.13.8: The post-Uruguay Round experience has been a mixed one for agricultural trade in India. In the ongoing negotiations on the Agreement on Agriculture, India submitted detailed proposals with a view to safeguarding the food and livelihood security of the large subsistence level farming community and maximising export opportunities for Indian agricultural products by seeking a reduction in the high tariffs and subsidies prevent in developed countries.

The Indian Parliament had passed the Protection of Plant Varieties and Farmers' Rights Act with the objective of giving a significant thrust to agricultural growth by providing an effective system for the protection of plant varieties and farmers' rights. This is expected to stimulate investments for research and development both in the public and the private sectors for the development of new plant varieties by ensuring appropriate returns on such investment.

A higher growth in agriculture, thus, needs a comprehensive revamp of agriculture policy with reorientation towards rapid diversification of this sector. A progressive correction is required in the incentive structure for agriculture so that the excessively high minimum support prices do not continue to distort resource allocation in agriculture. This will ensure that farmers diversify towards high value added segments of agriculture in response to the new demand structure.

Notes

1. Government of India, *Economic Survey*, 2000-2001, p. 166.
2. Reserve Bank of India, *Report on Currency and Finance*, 1998-99, p. III-8.
3. Government of India, *Economic Survey,* 1999-2000, p. 133.
4. Government of India, Planning Commission, *Seventh Five year Plan* (1985-86 to 1989-90), Vol. II, para 1.4.
5. Government of India, Planning Commission, *Eighth Five Year Plan* (1992-93 to 1996-97, p. 13.
6. Government of India, *Economic Survey,* 2000-2001, p. 170.
7. Reserve Bank of India, *Report on Currency and Finance,* 2001-02, p. VIII-2.
8. Government of India, Planning Commission, *An Approach to the Eleventh Five Year Plan,* November 2006, p. 5.
9. Ibid., p. 23.
10. Government of India, *Economic Survey,* 2001-02, p. 205.

2

Agricultural Finance: Sources and Policies

2.1 Introduction

Agricultural credit may be explained as the amount of investable funds made available for the purpose of development of farm productivity. According to the Agricultural Finance Corporation, it is the amount of money needed by a farmer to achieve a proper combination of productive factor, like, land, labour, inputs, machinery, livestock and managerial ability, so that the planned level of income is generated at his farm. It is true that credit alone cannot generate new resources, but credit is an important factor of integrated approach for improving production and productivity, marketing, land tenures, farmers' organisations and other aspects which are dependent on each other. Agricultural finance is not merely a subject of banking business. There is more to it than disbursing credit to farmers or fishermen. Though the amount of credit demanded by the individual borrower may be small but in aggregate, it represents considerable risks.

Most of the cultivators live just below the poverty line. Naturally, they tend to borrow money for conducting agricultural operations. These needy farmers should be helped with the sanction of credit as and when they require it. The paper work should be completed quickly. A strong foundation of agriculture is essential to maintain and continue the overall performance of agricultural sector in the economy and for socio-economic development in general.

In India, until 1980s, agricultural credit had been marked by predominance of non-institutional credit such as private moneylenders, traders, relatives, and similar individual lenders. Credit from these private sources is generally on unfavorable terms and therefore, farmers land in heavy debt adversely affecting the production. There are numerous instances of exploitation of the indebted farmers by the moneylenders. If farmers are to be given incentive for adopting improved farm practices, there must be institutional arrangements to supply all their credit needs.

Modern agriculture requires high quantum of credit. Various short-term cash inputs, like, use of improved seeds, fertilizers, insecticides etc., medium and long-term investment for irrigation, land improvements, etc., are compulsory for increasing agricultural production. Further, modern agriculture also requires co-ordination of various activities, like, appropriate estimate of credit, timely and adequate supply of inputs, repayment arrangements favorable to farmers, efficient machinery for recovery of loans and adequate marketing accommodations, etc. Introduction of institutional channel of credit is necessary to meet the increased needs.

2.2 Essential Features of Agricultural Credit

India is basically a rural economy and rural India virtually includes the cultivators, the village craftsmen and agricultural labourers. One of the serious and unrelenting problems faced by the Indian farmer's households has been the indebtedness. Despite substantial improvement in agricultural output and distribution of credit, still a majority of the farmers are suffering from this major economic malaise called indebtedness along with lack of timely and adequate farm credit. Agricultural distress witnessed in the country occasionally takes the form of suicides by farmers. It is a symptom of a deep-rooted malady arising from inadequate public investment and insufficient public action in recent years.

It is essential that a sound system of credit should be built up so as to fulfill the credit needs of the farmers and to ensure that agricultural credit serves the national economy in a dynamic way. Various criteria for a good credit system have been laid down by various experts and institutions. In this regard, the following criteria have been laid down by Lowis Tardy, a famous agricultural economist:

- The agricultural credit should be provided for a satisfactorily long period and it should be commensurate with the operations for which it is designed to facilitate.
- It should be provided at lower rate of interest.
- With a view to preventing the misuse of credit, it should be adequately secured but the security should not necessarily be material property.
- The credit should be granted against personal security of the borrower and on the basis of farming ability.
- Credit should be provided according to the average yield of the farms and capacity to repay, especially in times of economic depression.
- The credit should be provided through institutions, the officials of which have availed special training and have actual banking experience.

According to Reserve Bank of India (RBI), the credit system should have the following features: The credit system for modern agriculture should integrate the credit with services, like arrangements of inputs etc. which is better than facile credit, since because the farmer may use it for wasteful consumption purposes, which may impose an extra burden on the borrower. On the other hand, facile credit is more dangerous because it may lead the borrower to avail credit without any basic needs. Under the credit system, all areas and farmers (specially small and marginal farmers) should be covered. In other words, the credit system should be so efficient as to expand its activities horizontally as well as vertically. Under a good system of credit for modern agriculture, emphasis should be given to issue loans for production purposes. But the consumption loans should not be prohibited completely. The loans should be provided on the basis of anticipated production or increased income which would occur due to the use of credit rather than tangible security or existing income. It will help the small farmers to avail the credit and implement their own plan of cultivation. The cost of handling credit and services should be lower.

In the absence of this, most of the farmers will reject credit which may cause a burden beyond their repaying capacity. The credit system should be such which mobilises sufficient resources to provide finance for the purpose of investment required for modern agriculture. Some features of a sound agricultural credit system were determined by the All-India Rural Credit Survey Committee. These were: It should be associated with the possible support of the State. It should be an effective alternative to private sources of credit. It should have the strength of adequate resources and of well trained personnel. It should lend not merely on security of land and other usual forms of security but also on the security of anticipated crop yield. It should effectively supervise the use of credit and consequently bear in mind the borrower's legitimate needs and interests.

From the above discussion, suitable criteria for a good sound system of agricultural credit can be given as follows: All the credit needs – short, medium and long-term of the farmers should be met. Credit should be made available at door-step if as possible and when needed by the farmer. It should generate savings and accelerate economic growth. The borrower should be encouraged to adopt new technologies without which sufficient capital cannot be generated to repay loans. Supply and other services too should be made available to them. The lending agency should be geared to financing the entire farming system. The credit agency should be in a position to interlink with marketing agencies to ensure full recovery of loans.

Thus, in a good and sound system of agricultural credit there should be a provision for continuous evaluation of the credit programmers. This will assist to estimate quantitatively the impact on improvement in respect of farm production, cropping pattern, cropping intensity, farm output, employment opportunity and actual farm income. Under the sound credit system, guidance should be available to credit institutions in this regard from to time.

2.3 Period-based Classification of Agricultural Credit

Generally, agricultural credit may be classified into two types, namely direct and indirect. In direct type, credit is provided directly to farmers for productive purpose, such as, land improvement, irrigation, crop production, purchase of machinery, equipments, development of dairy, sheep rearing, poultry, fisheries, etc., development of plantation, tea, coffee, rubber, coconut, cashew nut, etc. Indirect type of agricultural credit is credit provided to the institutions involved in the supply of production inputs. The indirect credit is given for financing distribution of farm inputs like financing PACS/FSS /LAMPS/co-operative marketing societies, financing Regional Rural Bank (RRBs), financing State Electricity Board for energisation of pump sets, financing for service institutions that provide storage facilities, such as, godowns, cold storage and warehouses, financing for establishment of Regulated Markets, financing for Agro-Industries Corporation, Food Corporation of India, Jute Corporation of India, State Warehousing Corporation, etc. Most of the indirect finance is referred to as refinance. Agricultural credit may be further classified into the following ways.

2.3.1 Short-Term Credit: Short-term or seasonal credit is granted for the purpose of providing working capital requirement of the farmers. The period for which this type of credit is provided generally ranges from 6 months to 15 months. According to the All-India Rural Credit Review Committee, the short-term credit is lump sum credit facility, which is provided to fill up the gap in outlay which cannot be met by the own resource of farmers during the period between two harvests. The various purposes for which short-term credit is provided include purchase of seeds, fertilizers and insecticides, hiring of labour, hire charges of agricultural machineries, payment of electricity bills, tax on lands, godown charges, etc. The demand of this type of credit is expected to increase at the time of sowing/transplantation. This type of credit is also known as 'crop loans'. These loans are disbursed through Primary Agricultural Credit Societies (PACS), commercial banks and Regional Rural Banks (RRBs).

2.3.2 Medium-Term Credit: Medium-term credit is the credit required for improvement of land, purchase of implements, machinery, livestock and conversion of cultivation system. This credit is provided for more than 15 months but not exceeding 5 years.

2.3.3 Long-Terms Credit: The long-term loans are sanctioned for a longer period, i.e. more than 5 years up to 10 years. In some cases it may also be granted for a period up to 20 years. [22] Among the various types of uses of long-term loans, the principal ones are: purchase of farm or buying of additional land, construction of buildings for farm operations, provision of drainage, reclamation of land and other improvements.

2.4 Purpose-based Classification of Agricultural Credit

According to the Reserve Bank of India's classification, agricultural credits may be classified into three types, namely credit for farm business, non-farm business and family expenditure. Credit for farm business is meant for purchase of seeds, fertilizers, insecticides, hiring of labour, land improvements by irrigation and drainage, purchase of agricultural implements, machinery and livestock, construction of farm house, cattle shed, tanks and embankments, lying of orchards, etc. In other words, this credit is provided to support the working and capital expenses on farm business. In case of credit for non-farm business, credit is provided to meet the working capital expenses on non-farm business, such as, repair of production and transport equipment and furniture, purchase/construction and repair of buildings, purchase of non-farm equipments, etc. Credit for family expenditure includes credit to meet the household expenditures like, clothing, education, medicine, expenses regarding marriage, death ceremonies and other social events in family, litigation expenses, payment of old debts etc.

2.5 Other Bases of Classification of Agricultural Credit

2.5.1 Classification on the Basis of Security: Agricultural credit may be categorized as secured credit and unsecured credit. Secured credit includes 'farm mortgage credit' and 'Chattel or Collateral Credit'. The former is secured against some tangible property of the borrowers. In such cases, borrower's livestock, crops, warehouse receipts, shares, bonds, insurance policies, etc., are offered as security. Unsecured Credit is granted on the personal security of the borrowers. It is provided on the promissory or personal notes of the borrowers with or without guarantees.

2.5.2 Classification on the Basis of Creditor: The agricultural credit may be classified on the basis of creditor or lender also. There are two main sources of credit – Institutional and Non- Institutional. The former includes credit granted by co-operatives, commercial banks, RRBs, and the Government while the latter includes credit granted by moneylenders, commission agents, relatives and friends and others.

2.5.3 Classification on the Basis of Debtor: The borrowers, groups could be crop farmers, dairy farmers, poultry farmers, fishermen, etc.

2.6 Sources of Agricultural Credit

The financial requirements of the Indian farmers can be classified into three types depending upon the period and purpose for which they are required; the Indian farmers need funds for short periods of less than 15 months for the purpose of cultivation or for meeting domestic expenses. They require finance for medium period ranging between 15 months and 5 years for the purpose of making some improvement on land, buying cattle and agricultural implements. The farmers need finance for the purpose of buying additional land, to make permanent improvements on land and to purchase agricultural machinery. These loans are for long period of more than 5 years. For a long time, the major source of agricultural credit was the private money lenders. This source of credit was inadequate and highly expensive and exploitative. Since independence, a multi-agency approach consisting of co-operatives, commercial banks and regional rural banks-known as institutional credit has been adopted to provide cheaper and adequate credit to farmers.

Till Independence in 1947, money lenders and the landlords were the principal sources of rural credit. Over the years, the operations of moneylenders have declined in view of debt relief legislations, the system of licensing moneylenders and restrictions on the use and transfer of land as security. Similarly, the abolition of all privileged tenures both in zamindari and ryotwari areas has discouraged investment by the landlords and larger cultivators.

Agricultural growth is crucial for alleviating rural poverty. Access to institutional credit to more farmers and appropriate quantity and quality of agricultural credit are crucial for realising the full potential of agriculture as a profitable activity.

It is true that the institutional sources of credit have weakened the hold of moneylenders on the rural masses. However, the benefits of institutional credit have not percolated to all sections of rural population. Landless workers and marginal farmers have not benefited adequately due to their ignorance of new sources of credit and also on account of their weak repaying capacity. These underprivileged rural sections still depend on the moneylenders and suffer their exploitative practices.

The rising trend in private investment in agriculture was supported largely by institutional credit. The need for institutional credit arises because of the weakness or inadequacy of private agencies to supply credit to farmers. Institutional credit is not exploitative and the basic motive is always to help the farmers to raise his productivity and maximize his income. The rate of interest is not only relatively low but can be different for different groups of farmers and for different purposes. In the field of co-operation, the Primary Agricultural Credit Societies provide mainly short and medium term loans and Co-operative Agricultural and Rural Development Banks provide long term loans to the agricultural sector.

The commercial banks including Regional Rural Banks provide both short term and long term loans for agricultural and allied activities. The National Bank for Agriculture and Rural Development is the apex institution at the national level for agricultural credit and provides refinance assistance to primary lending institutions. The Reserve Bank of India plays a crucial role by giving overall direction to rural credit and financial support to NABARD for its operations.

Agricultural production in India depends upon millions of small farmers. It is the intensity of their effort and the efficiency of their technique that will help in raising yields per acre. Because of inadequate financial resources and absence of timely credit facilities at reasonable rates, many of the farmers, even though otherwise willing, are unable to go in for improved seeds and manures or to introduce better methods or techniques. It is, therefore, of the utmost importance that the financial requirements of the farmers are adequately met.

Provision of sufficient and timely credit at fair rates of interest has, therefore, to be considered as an integral part of agricultural development. Assistance rendered by way of credit has, however, to be related to specific items of productive work or of essential costs of cultivation.

2.6.1 Co-operative Societies: These societies form an integral part of the rural credit system in India. They are the main source of institutional credit to the farmers. These societies are chiefly responsible for breaking the monopoly of moneylenders in providing credit to the agriculturists. There are around 1 lakh such societies in the country at present.

In spite of their suitability and useful role in building up a just socio-economic rural life, co-operative societies suffer from various weaknesses. The heavy overdues of co-operative societies are a cause for concern. The rising overdues have reduced the borrowing and lending activities of these societies. Moreover, these societies have paid inadequate attention to the needs of landless workers and rural artisans. Influential people in the villages have been the main beneficiaries of co-operative credit. Of late, there has been a tendency on the part of political leadership to write-off loans of the farmers. The RBI has repeatedly expressed concern in this regard because non-repayment of loans by the existing borrowers can adversely affect recycling of funds and the credit chances of the prospective borrowers.

2.6.2 Micro Finance: Micro credit has emerged as a visible credit channel to the poor as their access to conventional credit channels is constrained by the requirement of collateral and high transaction cost. Micro finance is routed through self-help groups (SHGs). [1] The programme of linking self-help group (SHGs) of the rural poor with the banking system was launched as a pilot project in 1992. Over the years the SHG–bank linkage programme has emerged as the major microfinance programme in the country. 560 banks including 48 commercial banks, 196 RRBs and 316 co-operative banks are now actively involved in the operation of this programme. The focus under the Self-help Group (SHG) Bank Linkage Programme is largely on those rural poor who have no sustainable access to the formal banking system. The target groups, therefore, broadly comprise small and marginal farmers, agricultural and non-agricultural labourers, artisans and craftsmen and other poor engaged in small businesses like vending, and hawking.

The programme has been providing the rural poor access

to the formal banking system and has achieved several milestones in terms of gender sensitisation, empowerment and poverty alleviation. The programme provides thrift linked credit support to the members of SHGs. While the programme directly benefits the members, it also helps banks in reducing their transaction costs as well as risk in delivering small loans. The Union Budget for 2004-05 emphasised the need for promoting the programme more vigorously and for the graduation of SHGs from consumption or production credit to credit for starting micro enterprises. The Budget set an indicative target of credit linking 5.85 lakh SHGs by end-March, 2007.

The number of SHGs linked to banks reached 10.79 lakh by March 31, 2004, covering an estimated 167 lakh poor families. A redeeming feature of the programme is that 90 per cent of the groups linked with banks are exclusively women groups. Cumulative disbursements of bank loans to these SHGs amounted to Rs. 3,904 crore at end-March, 2004 with an average loan of Rs. 36,179 per SHG and Rs. 2,412 per family. Refinance support extended by NABARD amounted to Rs. 2,550 crore. During the year 2004-05, 1.97 lakh new SHGs were provided with bank loans amounting to Rs. 1,134 crore.

According to *Economic Survey, 2005-06*, "The 5,39,365 new self-help groups (SHGs) credit-linked during 2004-05 represented an increase of 49 per cent over the previous year. As on March 31, 2005, the total of 16.18 lakh SHGs credit-linked by banks covered an estimated 242 lakh poor families, with an average loan disbursement per family of Rs.3, 044. Refinance support extended by NABARD amounted to Rs. 3,082 crore. A highlight of the programme was that about 90 per cent of the groups linked with banks were exclusively women groups. As against the target of linking 3 lakh SHGs for the whole year 2005-06, 2.11 lakh new SHGs were linked by December 2005." [2]

The RBI has been taking a pro-active role in promoting micro-finance. It set up four Groups in 2002 to look into various aspects of micro-financing. Based on the recommendations made by these Groups, the RBI announced that banks should provide adequate incentives to their branches in making the procedures for financing the SHGs simple and easy. Based on the recommendations of the Vyas Committee (discussed below), the RBI, in its annual policy statement for 2004-05, indicated that micro-finance institutions would not be permitted to accept public deposits, unless they comply with the extant regulatory framework.

2.6.3 Kisan Credit Cards (KCCs): The Kisan credit cards (KCC) scheme, introduced in 1998-99, aims at providing crop loans to farmers in a flexible and cost-effective manner. The scheme is being implemented in all the States and Union Territories by all commercial banks, RRBs, state co-operative banks, central co-operative banks, and primary agricultural co-operative societies. Beneficiaries covered under the KCC are issued with a credit card and a pass book or a credit card-cum-pass book incorporating the name, address and particulars of land, borrowing limit, and the validity period. Production credit limits are fixed taking into account the entire production credit needs for a full year plus ancillary activities relating to crop production. Sub-limits are also fixed at the discretion of lending banks. Crop loan/short-term credit is in the form of a revolving cash credit facility involving any number of drawals and repayments within the limit fixed on the basis of operational land holding, cropping pattern and scale of finance.

Till recently, investment credit requirements of farmers remained outside the purview of KCC, causing additional cost and procedural inconvenience to farmers. To address these deficiencies in the KCC scheme, NABARD revised the scheme in August 2004 to cover term loans for agriculture and allied activities. Under the KCC, while the short-term as well as working capital credit is repayable in 12 months, the term loan is to be repaid within a maximum period of five years. Conversion/reschedulement of loans is permitted in case of damage to crops due to natural calamities. As on December 31,

2006, cumulative issue of KCCs amounted to 642.49 lakh (Table 2.1).

Table 2.1: Agency-wise Kisan Credit Cards (KCCs) Issued

(lakh)

Year	Cooperative banks	Regional rural banks (RRBs)	Commercial banks	Total
1998-99	1.56	0.06	6.22	7.84
1999-00	35.95	1.73	13.66	51.34
2000-01	56.14	6.48	23.90	86.52
2001-02	54.36	8.34	30.31	93.41
2002-03	45.79	9.64	27.00	82.43
2003-04	48.78	12.75	30.94	92.47
2004-05	35.56	17.29	43.95	96.80
2005-06	25.98	12.49	41.65	80.12
2006-07#	15.48	10.4	25.68	51.56
Total	**319.60**	**79.18**	**243.71**	**642.49**
% share	49.75	12.32	37.93	100.00

up to December 31, 2006.

Source: Government of India, *Economic Survey*, 2006-07, p. 66, Table 3.9.

At the instance of the RBI, the National Council of Applied Economic Research (NCAER) conducted a survey for assessing the impact of the KCC scheme. The survey has brought out several advantages of the KCC scheme in terms of increase in the flow of credit to the agriculture sector, reduction in borrowings from the informal sector, significant savings in time spent on obtaining credit and an overall reduction in cost of credit delivery. The survey had identified areas requiring policy initiatives to make the scheme more effective. These relate to restrictions imposed on the issuance of KCCs by banks, restrictions on use of KCCs only at card issuing branches, non-availability of incentives for timely repayments, low credit limits and low awareness regarding the provision of personal accident insurance scheme. The RBI has advised the Indian Banks Association to examine these suggestions and come up with remedial measures.

The kisan credit card scheme (KCC) has increased farmers' access to short term credit. The objective of the scheme is to provide adequate and timely support from the banking system to the farmers for their cultivation needs including purchases of inputs in a flexible and cost effective manner. Loans disbursed under KCCs are now covered under Rashtriya Krishi Beema Yojna of the General Insurance Corporation. KCC holders are being provided personal accident insurance cover of Rs. 50,000 for accidental death and Rs. 25,000 for permanent disability. The RBI in its Annual Policy Statement had indicated that a survey would be conducted to assess the impact of the scheme on the beneficiaries. Accordingly, preparatory work has been initiated to conduct the survey with the help of an outside agency.

The introduction of Kisan Credit Cards (KCCs) was a significant innovation in the rural credit delivery mechanism. However, the outreach of the KCCs to cover all eligible farmers under the scheme has been hampered by the lack of updated land records, small landholdings and illiteracy of borrowers.

According to *Economic Survey*, 2005-06, "The growing popularity of the KCC scheme reflects its effectiveness in ensuring hassle-free and timely operations as also availability of credit with minimum transaction cost and documentation.

In order to safeguard the interests of the KCC holders for coverage under Personal Accident Insurance Scheme (PAIS) on an ongoing basis on competitive terms, NABARD has allowed discretion to the banks to opt for "any insurance company of their choice". This facilitates personal accident insurance coverage on an ongoing basis, at competitive rates/terms. With a view to meet credit needs of the farmers through a single window, NABARD has enlarged the scope of the KCC, beyond the existing facility of providing crop loan limit, to cover term loans for agriculture and allied activities, including a reasonable component of consumption needs." [3]

2.6.4 Moneylenders: There are two types of moneylenders in rural areas: (a) agriculturist moneylenders who carry on the business of money lending along with farming, and (b) professional moneylenders whose only occupation is money lending. Although the relative importance of moneylenders has declined over the years, they are still an important source of credit for the rural people, particularly the small farmers and the artisans.

Moneylenders are popular because, unlike government agencies, they give credit for every purpose. They are easily approachable by the credit seekers and there are not many formalities in transacting a loan. However, the malpractices adopted by the moneylenders to exploit the needy farmers cannot be overlooked. These malpractices pertain to charging of high rate of interest and adopting unfair means in the maintenance of accounts.

2.7 Advisory Committee on the Flow of Credit to Agriculture and Related Activities from the Banking System (Chairman: V.S. Vyas), 2004

As indicated in its mid-term review of November, 2003, the RBI constituted an Advisory Committee on flow of Credit to Agriculture and Related Activities from the Banking System (Chairman: V.S. Vyas). The Advisory Committee submitted its interim report in April, 2004 and the final report in June, 2004. It made the following recommendations.

- A review of mandatory lending to agriculture by commercial banks to enlarge direct lending programmes.
- Public and private sector banks to increase their direct agricultural lending to 12 per cent of net bank credit in the next two years and to 13.5 per cent two years thereafter, within the overall limit of 18.0 per cent of total agricultural lending.
- Banks to increase their disbursements to small and marginal farmers under Special Agricultural Credit Plan

(SACP) to 40 per cent by March 2007.

- SACP to be restricted to direct lending and extended to private sector banks.
- Reduction in cost of agricultural credit by enhancing the cost effectiveness of agricultural loans.
- NPA norms for agricultural credit to be aligned with crop seasons. Loans for allied activities to be classified as NPA after 180 days of default. Credit flow to small borrowers to be improved through reduction in cost of borrowing, revolving credit packages, procedural simplification, involvement of Panchayati Raj institutions and micro-finance.
- The SAA to be modified to remove rigidities. SAA to be mandatory only for Government sponsored programmes and the format of village surveys to be changed in view of current realities.

Based on the recommendations contained in the interim report of the Vyas Committee, the RBI, in its annual policy statement for 2004-05, announced a number of measures to improve credit delivery to agriculture. These included, treating loans to storage units designed to store agricultural products, irrespective of location, as indirect credit to agriculture, treating investment by banks in securitised assets representing direct (indirect) lending to agriculture as direct (indirect) lending to agriculture, and waiver of margin/security requirement for agricultural loans up to Rs. 50,000 and in case of agribusiness and agri-clinics for loans up to Rs. 5 lakh. In addition, RBI also aligned repayment dates with harvesting of crops by treating loans granted for short duration crops as an NPA, if the instalment of the principal or interest thereon remains unpaid for two crop seasons beyond the due date. Loans granted for long duration crops are treated as an NPA, only if the instalment of the principal or interest thereon remains unpaid for one crop season beyond the due date.

As recommended by the Vyas Committee, RBI announced that microfinance institutions would not be permitted to accept public deposits, unless they comply with the extant regulatory framework. The recommendation relating to service area approach (SAA) was accepted and an announcement to this effect was made in the RBI's mid-term review of annual policy statement for 2004-05.

Recently, most of the PSBs, co-operative banks and RRBs have reduced the rate of interest on farm loans up to Rs. 50,000 to 9.0 per cent and, in some cases, to 8.5 per cent. This has enabled the farmers to derive the benefit of falling interest rates and to improve their margins on farming and allied operations. Also, as a measure to minimise the incidence of under-financing, the scale of finance for crop loans and unit costs of farm investments have been further revised and made more realistic in the current year. Furthermore, to mitigate the risk of agriculture arising out of drought conditions, banks either postponed the recovery of loans or converted short-term credit into medium-term credit with appropriate reschedulement in repayment in the concerned areas. The norms of financing in the Rabi season have been liberalised taking into account the likely shortfall in Kharif output on account of deficient rainfall.

In connection with the implementation of the recommendations of the Vyas Committee, the *Economic Survey, 2005-06* observed, "Continuing its endeavour to enhance the flow of credit to agriculture by removing delivery bottlenecks, the RBI, together with NABARD, implemented most of the recommendations of the Advisory Committee on Flow of Credit to Agriculture and Related Activities from the Banking System (Chairman: Prof. V.S. Vyas). Out of 99 recommendations made by the Committee, 33 were accepted and implemented by October 2005. These related to the following matters.

- Procedural modifications and rationalisation of systems and procedures.
- Tie-ups with related farm machinery manufacturers by banks.

- Use of a flexible revolving credit limit to small borrowers of production or investment loans for meeting temporary shortfalls in family cash flows.
- Co-opting joint liability group (JLG) and self-help group (SHG) approaches in addressing issues relating to financing oral lessees.
- Addressing delays/refusal in opening savings bank accounts of SHGs.
- Improving staffing in the rural areas to promote retail lending to agriculture.
- Use of individual volunteers, farmers' clubs or NGOs/SHGs as direct selling agents.
- Building synergy between good working primary agricultural credit societies and commercial banks.
- Use of IT in rural branches.
- Working out appropriate incentive structure for prompt repayment.
- Making the rates of interest on small loans reasonable.
- Improving the efficiency of credit delivery to small borrowers and association with contract farming.

Furthermore, some of the recommendations, *viz.*, stepping up credit for marketing and introduction of negotiable warehousing receipt system, support of State Governments for collecting dues, reduction of stamp duty on agricultural loans, legal amendments to Agricultural Produce Marketing Committee (APMC) Act by the State Governments, amendment to NABARD Act for operational autonomy, which were referred to the Government of India for examination, have been accepted." [4]

2.8 Expert Group on Investment Credit (Chairman: Y.S.P. Thorat), 2005

With a view to increasing the flow of credit to agriculture, the RBI set up this Expert Group to formulate a strategy for increasing investment credit in agriculture. The Group in its Report submitted in June 2005 identified several factors which constrain growth in investment in agriculture. These included the following.

- Meagre growth in minor irrigation and farm mechanization.
- Declining public sector investment.
- Limited credit absorptive capacity.
- Lack of effective mechanism for technology transfer and poor extension services.
- Inadequate extension services.
- Limited infrastructure for agro processing, storage, warehousing, value addition and marketing.
- Restrictions on purchases outside the *mandis*.
- Weather aberrations and output price fluctuations.
- Inadequate risk mitigation mechanism.
- Non-availability of land records.

The Group emphasised the need to accelerate investment in agriculture in order to achieve the desired level of growth. It also highlighted the need for investments to be appropriately structured, timed and well implemented in order to attain maximum effectiveness.

Major recommendations of the Group are set out below.

1. In view of various changes in the Indian rural canvas over the past few years, there is need for a shift in the thrust areas for investment credit to agriculture. Apart from the traditional investments such as land development and irrigation, increased focus needs to be accorded to the entire supply chain management of agriculture products, reform of agriculture markets and public management in agricultural infrastructure.
2. State Governments need to lay emphasis on legal provisions/computerisation of land records, legal support for recovery, reforms in agricultural marketing, improving credit absorptive capacity through supporting infrastructure, strengthening infrastructure, improving extension network and developing marketing links.

3. NABARD should take special steps to facilitate capacity building of credit institutions in appraisal skill, particularly in North Eastern States, and design appropriate products for financing rural infrastructure projects outside the RIDF by mobilising resources from the market or banks at competitive rates of interest.
4. Water management policies and investment in water conservation be designed jointly by the State Governments and banks for improving productivity in agriculture.
5. The State Governments and NABARD should make investments in participatory community projects and in soil treatment to make wasteland and fallow land cultivable.
6. With a view to strengthening the institutional credit mechanism, short-term credit be integrated with term credit and efforts be made to reach the 'unreached' areas, promote supplementary credit delivery channels, outsource monitoring services, provide loan support for diversified agriculture, review HR policies, share the pool of technical expertise and make use of the model bankable projects prepared by NABARD.
7. The RBI along with banks could adopt agency models for credit delivery,
8. Government of India/State Governments and organisations engaged in agricultural research and development (R&D) to reorient R&D activities.
9. To mitigate the risk in financing of agriculture, the Group suggested several measures. These included:

- developing suitable financial products and commodity exchanges;
- allowing banks to operate on behalf of farmers and participate in commodity futures;
- establishing a risk fund for fragile agriculture;
- designing special risk mitigation packages for low asset-based borrowers;
- using warehousing receipts with price hedging

instruments;
- adopting technology for dissemination of market intelligence;
- sharing borrower information; and
- financing value chain by banks/through RIDF.

2.9 Group to Examine Issues Relating to Rural Credit and Micro-finance (Chairman: H.R. Khan), 2005

As a follow-up to the announcement in the Union Budget, 2005-06, the RBI constituted this Internal Group which in its Report submitted in July 2005 observed that there is an imperative need to work out efficient mechanisms involving external entities to cater to the under-serviced areas and the rural poor.

The Group felt that extended outreach to the under-serviced areas and the rural poor would facilitate acquisition of a large number of customers, *albeit* small ones with substantial potential for large increase in business volumes and profit as banking with the poor is rather profitable banking. The major recommendations of the Group are set out below.

1. For providing comprehensive financial services encompassing savings, credit and remittance, insurance and pension products in rural areas, the Group recommended two models, *viz.*, the Business Facilitator Model and the Business Correspondent Model as proactive response.
2. Under the Business Facilitator Model, it was envisaged that banks could use a wide array of civil society organisations (CSOs) and others for supporting them by undertaking non-financial services. The Facilitators would provide support services for effective delivery of financial services such as (a) borrower identification, (b) collection, processing and submission of applications, (c) preliminary appraisal, (c) marketing of the financial products including savings, (d) post-sanction monitoring, (e) promotion and nurturing SHGs/Joint Liability Groups (JLGs) and (f)

follow-up for recovery.

3. NGOs, farmers clubs, functional co-operatives, IT enabled rural outlets of corporates, postal agents, insurance agents, well-functioning panchayats, rural multi-purpose kiosks/village knowledge centres, agri-clinics/business centers financed by banks, Krishi Vigyan Kendras, Khadi and Village Industry Commission (KVIC)/ Khadi and Village Industries Commission Board (KVIB) units may function as the Business Facilitators.
4. Under the Business Correspondent Model, institutional agents/other external entities may support the banks for extending financial services. The Business Correspondents would function as "pass through" agencies to provide credit related services such as disbursal of small value credit, recovery of principal/ collection of interest and sale of micro insurance/mutual fund products/pension products besides the other functions of Business Facilitator Model.
5. Registered NBFCs with significant rural presence, NGO-micro-finance institutions (MFIs) set up under the Societies/Trust Act, Mutually Aided Co-operative Societies (MACS) with a charter to undertake financial functions, IT enabled rural outlets of corporates with appropriate contractual agreements with the principal, well running primary agricultural credit societies (PACSs) and post offices may function as the Business Correspondents.
6. The micro credit portfolio of the regulated MFIs may be made eligible for direct finance from NABARD; a line of credit may be extended by NABARD to provide liquidity assistance in view of the co-variant nature of credit risk of the MFIs.
7. Institutions such as NABARD and SIDBI may provide bulk lending support to start-up MFIs and funds of State/ Central Development/Finance Corporations, if feasible, may be channelised through NABARD to identified MFIs.
8. Accounting standards for SHGs and NGOs may be developed, codified, and standardised by NABARD as a

promotional initiative in consultation with the Institute of Chartered Accountant of India (ICAI).

9. NABARD, in consultation with Ministry of Information and Technology, may draw up a time bound action plan to set up Rural Kiosks/ Village Knowledge Centers, partly funded from RIDF. The remaining cost may be borne by the Central/State Governments on a shared basis.
10. The MFIs may be rated to help banks/financial institutions to decide about engaging them as their agents and funding them. The rating agencies need to be accredited with an appropriate authority.
11. NABARD, SIDBI and major banks may consider promoting independent rating agencies by way of equity contributions. Financial support may be provided to the accredited rating agencies to cover their operational deficits for a period of three to five years and the expenses in this regard may be met from the Micro Finance Development and Equity Fund (MFDEF).
12. Non-deposit taking MFIs may attempt self-regulation by forming State level associations.
13. A separate and exclusive regulatory and supervisory framework for MFIs may not be required for the present.
14. Considering the high transaction costs and the emphasis on timely availability of credit, it may not be appropriate to fix any ceiling on interest rates and service fees charged by MFIs.

2.10 Working Group on Warehouse Receipts and Commodity Futures (Chairman: Prashant Saran), 2005

In pursuance of the announcement made in the Mid-term Review of Annual Policy Statement for the year 2004-05, the RBI constituted this Working Group with a view to examining the role of banks in providing loans against warehouse receipts and evolving a framework for participation of banks in the commodity futures market. The Working Group in its Report submitted in April 2005 recommended that banks may be permitted to offer futures-based products to farmers in order to enable them to hedge against price risk.

The Working Group was entrusted with the task of evolving broad guidelines, criteria, limits, risk management system as also a legal framework for facilitating participation of banks in commodity (derivative) market and use of warehouse receipts in financing of agriculture. The major recommendations of the Group are set out below.

1. As banks at present are not allowed to deal in goods, the Central Government may issue a Notification under clause (o) of sub-section (1) of Section 6 of the Banking Regulation Act, 1949 permitting banks to deal in the business of agricultural commodities, including derivatives.
2. Considering the experience that banks already have in dealing with agricultural commodities, it would be prudent at the current stage to permit banks to deal with derivatives in agricultural commodities only.
3. A system needs to be evolved by which warehouse receipts become freely transferable between holders as it would reduce transaction costs and increase usage.
4. An umbrella structure, which may act as a Closed User Group (CUG) for everyone engaged in the agricultural commodities business, be created. The umbrella structure is envisaged as an electronic platform that would offer straight through processing for everyone connected with commodities. There can be more than one CUG which would be subject to regulation and supervision by a regulatory authority such as Forward Markets Commission (FMC).
5. Proprietary positions in agricultural commodity derivatives could be used by banks to mitigate their risk in lending to farmers. To achieve this, they will have to buy options on futures.
6. The Forward Contracts (Regulation) Act, 1952 be amended and the FMC should evolve a framework for

introducing "options" trading in agricultural commodities in India.

7. Banks may be permitted to have independent proprietary position in commodity futures linked in a macro way to their credit portfolio. However, suitable risk control measures may have to be adopted by banks.
8. At present, purely cash-settled contracts are not available in India. The banks trading or dealing in commodity contracts should, therefore, be prepared to make or accept delivery of physical goods. While no restriction may be placed in this regard, banks may be persuaded to preferably close their positions and cash settle the contracts.
9. Banks may be granted general permission to become professional clearing members of commodity exchanges subject to the condition that they do not assume any exposure risk on account of offering clearing services to their trading clients. At least for the present, banks may not be permitted to act as trading members in the commodity exchanges.
10. While banks may continue to hold their equity stake in the commodity exchanges in order to provide them financial strength and stability, they may reduce/divest their equity holding to a maximum permitted level of 5 per cent over a period of time so as to avoid any conflict of interest.

2.11 Agricultural Credit: Recent Policy Announcements

Credit flow to agriculture sector from all formal sources amounted to Rs. 70,810 crore in 2002-03 and Rs. 86,981 crore in 2003-04, much below the levels envisaged in the Tenth Plan. Concerned over the slower growth of agriculture credit, the Government announced a comprehensive policy on June 18, 2004. The policy envisages a 30 per cent increase in credit to agriculture sector in 2004-05 over an estimated credit flow of Rs. 80,000 crore in 2003-04. The implementation of the policy has been entrusted to public sector banks, private sector banks, regional rural banks (RRBs) and co-operative banks. The policy has indicated that each rural and semi-urban branch of commercial banks, on an average, will take up at least two to three new investment projects in the area of plantation and horticulture, fisheries, organic farming, agro-processing, livestock, micro irrigation, sprinkler irrigation, watershed management, village pond development and other agricultural activities. NABARD has been asked to advise District Level Technical Committees to review the scales of finance to meet the realistic credit needs of farmers, especially for capital intensive agricultural operations.

In short, Government took the following steps to boost credit flow to the agricultural sector

- To step up agricultural credit from all lending institutions, estimated at Rs. 80,000 crore during the 2003-04, by 30 per cent to around Rs. 1,05,000 crore during 2004-05.
- The share of various agencies shall be as follows: (a) commercial banks: Rs. 57,000 crore, (b) regional rural banks: Rs. 8,500 crore and (c) cooperative banks: Rs. 39,000 crore
- The branches of CBs and RRBs will be energized to enhance the flow of agricultural credit.
- Under special agricultural credit plan, at least 100 new farmers should be financed at each rural and semi-urban branch during the current year, resulting in enrolment of about 50 lakh new borrowers.¨
- Financing of at least 2 to 3 new investment projects by each branch in plantation and horticulture, fisheries, organic farming, etc.
- Financing at least 10 Agro Clinics in each district during the current year.
- Providing credit to tenant farmers and oral lessees.
- Revisiting of scales of finance and re-aligning the same to meet the realistic needs of the farmers, especially
- capital-intensive agricultural operations.
- Special packages to promote technological upgradation in

agriculture, agro-processing and agri-biotech.

- Debt restructuring as opposed to debt writes off in the following forms: (a) relief to farmers in distress by restructuring/rescheduling of their loans and making them eligible for fresh loans, (b) rescheduling of the debts of farmers in arrears and making them eligible for fresh loans, (c) one Time Settlement (OTS) for small and marginal farmers and consider them eligible for fresh loans and (d) redemption of past debts from non-institutional lenders.

The Budget for 2004-05, presented in the Parliament on July 8, 2004, proposed doubling of credit to agriculture in three years and announced further measures to achieve the target growth in agricultural credit. These measures include holding the sponsor bank of each RRB squarely responsible for the performance of RRB under its control and an incentive scheme under which RRBs adopting new governance standards and abiding by prudential regulations will qualify for receiving funds from the Government for their restructuring. The Budget proposed setting up of a Task Force to examine the reforms required in the cooperative banking system including the appropriate regulatory regime.

The Union Finance Minister while presenting the 2005-06 budget to the Parliament made the following observations regarding rural credit and indebtedness, "Government intends to continue with its effort to turn the focus of commercial banks, regional rural banks (RRBs) and cooperative banks towards providing credit, especially production credit, to rural households and farm households. Particularly in agricultural credit, innovations are possible. I propose to request the Reserve Bank of India (RBI) to examine the issue of allowing banks to adopt the agency model, by using the infrastructure of civil society organizations, rural kiosks and village knowledge centres, to provide credit support to rural and farm sectors.

In June 2004, I had announced my intention to double the flow of agricultural credit in three years. I had also announced an indicative target of Rs. 105,000 crore. Notwithstanding a below par performance by co-operative banks, together, all three arms will disburse Rs. 108,500 crore in the current year. Continuing on the same path, I propose to ask commercial banks, RRBs and cooperative banks to increase the flow of credit by another 30 per cent in 2005-06. Further, the public sector banks would be asked to increase the number of borrowers by another 50 lakh." [4]

2.11.1 Agricultural Credit in the 2006-07 Union Budget: In his 2006-07 budget speech, the Union Finance Minister made the following announcements regarding agricultural credit, "Farm credit increased to Rs.125,309 crore in 2004-05 (well above the target) and is again expected to cross the target of Rs.141,500 crore set for the current year. I propose to ask the banks to increase the level of credit to Rs.175,000 crore in 2006-07 and also add another 50 lakh farmers to their portfolio. We shall not only achieve but exceed the target of doubling farm credit in three years. Since tenant farmers are not adequately served, I have asked the banks to open a separate window for self-help groups or joint liability groups of tenant farmers and ensure that a certain proportion of the total credit is extended to them. I intend to monitor closely progress in this behalf...For our farmers, I have more. Farmers obtain short-term credit from the cooperative credit structure and Regional Rural Banks (RRBs), with refinance from NABARD. Increasingly, scheduled commercial banks are also lending more to farmers. It is my intention to ensure that NABARD continues to provide refinance at an economical rate, so that the farmer ultimately gets the loan at a reasonable rate. Accordingly, after giving anxious consideration to market conditions, Government has decided to ensure that the farmer receives short-term credit at 7 per cent, with an upper limit of Rs.300,000 on the principal amount. This would require a certain level of subvention to NABARD. I propose to give the subvention. This policy will come into force with effect from Kharif 2006-07, and I shall make a detailed statement in due course." [5]

As a result of above policy measures, the flow of institutional credit to the agricultural sector has increased significantly in recent years (Table 2.2).

Table 2.2: Flow of Institutional Credit to Agriculture in Recent Years

(Rs. crore)

Agency	2000-01	2001-02	2002-03	2003-04	2004-05	2005-06
Cooperative banks	20,800	23,604	23,176	26,959	30,639	28,947
RRBs	4,220	4,854	6,070	7,581	11,718	11,146
Commercial banks	27,807	33,587	39,774	52,441	72,886	77,806
Total	52,827	62,045	69,560	86,981	1,15,243	117899

*Up to December 31 2005.

Source Government of India, Economic Survey, 2005-06, Table 8.13, p. 165.

2.12 Financial Inclusions

Indian economy in general and banking services in particular have made rapid strides in the recent past. However, a sizeable section of the population, particularly the vulnerable groups, such as weaker sections and low income groups, continue to remain excluded from even the most basic opportunities and services provided by the financial sector. To address the issue of such financial exclusion in a holistic manner, it is essential to ensure that a range of financial services is available to every individual. These services are a no-frills banking account for making and receiving payments, a savings product suited to the pattern of cash flows of a poor household, money transfer facilities, small loans and overdrafts for productive, personal and other purposes and micro-insurance (life and non-life)

In order to address the issues of financial inclusion, the Government of India constituted a "Committee on Financial Inclusion" under the Chairmanship of Dr. C. Rangarajan. The Committee submitted its Final Report to Hon'ble Union

Finance Minister on January 4, 2008. The Committee has defined Financial Inclusion as "The process of ensuring access to financial services and timely and adequate credit where needed by vulnerable groups such as weaker sections and low income groups at an affordable cost."

The major recommendations of the Committee include, Launching of a National Rural Financial Inclusion Plan in mission mode with a clear target to provide access to comprehensive financial services including credit to at least 50 per cent (say 55.77 million) of the financially excluded rural cultivator/non-cultivator households, by 2012 through rural/semi-urban branches of Commercial Banks and Regional Rural Banks.

The remaining households have to be covered by 2015.For the purpose, a National Mission on Financial Inclusion is proposed to be constituted comprising representatives from all stakeholders to aim at achieving universal financial inclusion within a specific time frame, Constitution of two funds with NABARD, one is the Financial Inclusion Promotion and Development Fund and other one is the Financial Inclusion Technology Fund with an initial corpus of Rs. 500 crore each to be contributed by Government of India, Reserve Bank of India and NABARD.

The Financial Inclusion Promotion and Development Fund will focus on interventions like, Farmers' Service Centers, Promoting Rural Entrepreneurship, Self-Help Groups and their Federations, Developing Human Resources of Banks, Promotion of Resource Centers and Capacity Building of Business Facilitators and Correspondents, while the Financial Inclusion Technology Fund will focus on funding of low-cost technology solutions, Deepening the outreach of microfinance programme through financing to Self Help Groups and Joint Liability Groups and setting up of a risk mitigation mechanism for lending to small marginal farmers/share croppers/tenant farmers through Joint Liability Groups, Use of Primary Agriculture Credit Societies as Business Facilitators and

Correspondents, Micro finance – Non Banking Finance Companies could be permitted to provide thrift, credit, micro-insurance, remittances and other financial services up to a specified amount to the poor in rural, semi-urban and urban areas.

Such Micro finance-Non Banking Finance Companies may also be recognized as Business Correspondents of banks for providing only savings and remittance services and also act as micro insurance agents, Opening of specialized microfinance branches, cells in potential urban centers for exclusively catering to microfinance and Self Help Groups - bank linkages requirements of the urban poor. An enabling provision is made in the NABARD Act, 1981 permitting NABARD to provide micro finance services to the urban poor.

Notes

1. The concept of self-help groups (SHGs) was promoted by NABARD in 1991-92. The objective is to meet the financial needs of the poor by linking self-help groups with the formal credit agencies.

2. Government of India, *Economic Survey, 2005-06*, p. 5.

3. Ibid., p. 64.

4. Government of India, Ministry of Finance, Budget Papers, 2005-06, *Speech of Minister of Finance*, p. 10.

5. Government of India, Ministry of Finance, Budget Papers, 2006-07, *Speech of Minister of Finance*, p. 9.

3

NABARD: Functions and Working

3.1 Development Banking in India

The history of agricultural development banking in India is a story of a newly independent Nation which was predominantly agricultural with vast numbers of resource-poor farmers caught in a cycle of low productivity and low investment that the bankers had ignored for decades. Observers in the West were ready to write off India as a basket case, incapable of feeding itself. The far reaching developments in the last thirty years of Indian agriculture have their origin in a combined effort launched by the Government, the bankers and the scientists of India.

The concept of development banking in the Indian context rests essentially on the proactive involvement of the banks and other promotional agencies in tapping the potential opportunities of underdeveloped sectors and groups. For this purpose, development banks have to assume the role of a gap-filler by providing supplementary finance. Agricultural Refinance and Development Corporation (ARDC), thus had to provide long term refinance for agricultural development projects which could not be financed on their own by the credit agencies either because of the large outlays involved or because the project could not be brought within their normal rules of business. There was the greater need to induce the commercial banks for long-term credit support through development banking. These banks were reluctant to deploy resources for long term purposes in agricultural lending for reasons, such as, lower margins, longer repayment periods, and the general uncertainty due to the frequent occurrence of natural calamities. Under these circumstances, it was necessary to motivate the commercial banks by offering refinance support to them to meet the long term credit requirement of the farm sector.

Under the conventional banking practices characterized by security oriented lending; the ability of a large number of farmers to attract finance would be strictly limited by the ownership of entrepreneurial capital. This approach would have resulted in aggravating the already skewed distribution of land and other resources. Development banking, therefore, had to intervene to correct such imbalances by providing credit support to a large number of resource-scarce farmers. The nationalization of the major commercial banks was intended, among other things, to promote the objective of reaching credit to smaller customers in different sectors. This was all the more important for the rapid adoption by the small farmers of the high yielding seed fertilizer technology which is assize neutral technology. Another case for promoting development banking in the rural sector arises from the influence it exerts on the operation of the informal credit market. The latter has been exercising a significant hold on rural borrowers, especially, on small and marginal cultivators and loosening of its hold would be to the advantage of the weaker sections.

A necessary role expected of developmental banking in India is the reduction of regional imbalances. Some regions develop faster than others which tend to lag behind due to neglect, poor appreciation of their resource potential or insufficient response of the large numbers of tradition-bound and illiterate farmers to any fresh development initiative. The need arises for development banking under such situations to adopt different strategies in credit-supported agricultural development. Developmental banks have to do a great deal of promotional work to extend financial assistance and ensure its optimum use.

3.2 Genesis and History of NABARD

Reserve Bank of India, at the instance of Government of India appointed a 'Committee to Review Arrangements for

Institutional Credit for Agriculture and Rural Development' (CRAFICARD) in 1979 under the chairmanship of Shri B. Sivaraman. With a view to having a fresh look at the arrangements in existence for agricultural credit, the Committee sought to review/examine, inter alia, the structure and operations of Agricultural Refinance Development Corporation (ARDC) in the context of an increasing need for term-loans for agriculture and the feasibility of integrating short-term and medium-term credit structure with long-term credit structure at national, state, district and village levels.

The CRAFICARD felt that certain inherent handicaps inhibited the effectiveness of the national level institutions in meeting the gigantic task of integrated rural development which aimed at the enlistment of the weaker sections in the rural areas, within a given time frame. In this context, the Committee recommended the formation of a National Bank for Agriculture and Rural Development as a national level organization to provide undivided attention, forceful direction and pointed focus to the credit problems arising out of the integrated approach to rural development. The proposal was approved by Government of India and Reserve Bank of India and the National Bank of Agriculture and Rural Development Act, 1981, were passed by the Parliament. National Bank for Agriculture and Rural Development (NABARD) was established on 12 July 1982 by an Act of Parliament. The agriculture credit functions of the Reserve Bank of India (RBI) and refinance functions of the then Agriculture Refinance and Development Corporation (ARDC) were transferred to NABARD on its formation.

The Mandate of NABARD was setup by the Government of India as Development Bank with the objective of facilitating credit flow for promotion and development of agriculture, small-scale industries, cottage and village industries, handicrafts and other rural crafts. It also has the mandate to support all other allied economic activities in rural areas, promote integrated and sustainable rural development and secure prosperity of rural areas, as also for matters connected therewith and incidental thereto.

3.3 Role and Mission of NABARD

The main role of NABARD is facilitating credit flow for agriculture, rural infrastructure and rural development, promoting and supporting policies, practices and innovations conducive to rural development, strengthening rural credit delivery system through institutional development and supervising Rural Financial Institutions (Co-operative Banks and Regional Rural Banks). The mission of the NABARD is to promote sustainable and equitable agriculture and rural prosperity through effective credit support, related services, institutional development and other innovative initiatives

3.3.1 Objectives: NABARD was established in terms of the Preamble to the Act for providing credit for the promotion of agriculture, small scale industries, cottage and village industries, handicrafts and other rural crafts and other allied economic activities in rural areas with a view to promoting IRDP and securing prosperity of rural areas and for matters connected therewith. The main objectives of the NABARD as stated in the statement of objectives while placing the Bill before the Lok Sabha were categorized as, "The National Bank will be an apex organization in respect of all matters relating to policy, planning, operational aspects in the field of credit for promotion of agriculture, small scale industries, cottage and village industries, handicrafts and other rural crafts and other allied economic activities in rural areas. The Bank will serve as a refinancing institution for institutional credit, both long-term and short-term for the promotion of activities in the rural areas. The Bank will also provide direct lending to any institution as may be approved by the Central Government and the Bank will have organic links with the Reserve Bank and maintain a close link with in".

The main activity of NABARD is preparing of Potential Linked Credit Plans for identification of exploitable potential under agriculture and other activities available for development through bank credit and refinance to banks for extending loans for investment and production purpose in rural areas. Providing loans to State Government/ Non Government Organization, Panchayati Raj Institutions for developing rural infrastructure, supporting non-government organizations and other non-formal agencies through credit innovations schemes, extending formal banking services to the rural poor by evolving a supplementary credit delivery strategy in a cost effective manner by promoting Self-help Groups. Promoting participatory watershed development for enhancing productivity and profitability of rain fed agriculture in a sustainable manner, providing consultancy services related to agriculture, rural development and rural finance and on-site inspection of cooperative banks and Regional Rural Banks and off-site surveillance over health of cooperative and Regional Rural Banks are few other objectives of NABARD.

3.3.2 Functions: The functions of NABARD are classified as credit planning and monitoring, financial services, promotion and development and supervision functions. The credit planning and monitoring function includes preparation of district-wise annual credit plans indicating exploitable potential available for development through bank credit under agriculture, allied activities, rural non-farm sector, etc., preparation of state focus paper based on Potential Linked Credit Plans (PLPs), formulation of policies and operational guidelines for Rural Financial Institutions (RFIs), and monitoring the flow of ground level credit. The function relating to financial services includes refinancing Rural Financial Institutions for financing investment and production purposes in rural areas, loans to State Governments for strengthening co-operatives and also developing critical infrastructure including social infrastructure in rural areas, support for micro-credit innovations of Non-Governmental Organizations (NGOs) and other non-formal agencies and monitoring and evaluation of financed projects.

In case of promotion and development functions, it deals with institutional development of client organizations, capacity building of partner institutions, support experimentation with new models and practices in development and credit delivery, dissemination of innovative products and ideas, supporting Research and Development (R&D), assisting Reserve Bank of India or Government of India in formulation of policies relating to rural credit, promotion of Rural Non-Farm Sector (RNFS), promotion of Kisan Credit Card (KCC), promotion of Farmers' Clubs, Joint Liability Groups and Tenant Farmers, promotion of micro-credit innovations and consultancy services. The supervision function includes on-site inspection of Cooperative Banks and Regional Rural Banks and off-site surveillance of the health of Cooperative Banks and Regional Rural Banks.

NABARD's functions are further classified into credit planning, credit products and clients short-term credit. Under credit planning, NABARD prepares planning for district, State and National level. Under district level function, NABARD prepares Potential Linked Credit Plans annually for all the districts in the country. It assesses the potential available for development in agriculture and rural sectors in the districts and projects the credit requirements, taking into account the long-term physical potential, availability of infrastructure, extension services, marketing support and the strengths and weaknesses of the Rural Financial Institutions. The PLP forms the basic for preparation of District Credit Plan at the district level by banks from 2006-07.

In case of State level function, NABARD prepares State Focus Papers for each state, which presents, interalia, a comprehensive picture of the potential available in the State for development of agriculture and allied sectors and also critical gaps in infrastructure and support services. It is used by the bankers, State Government and other agencies for preparing their plans for investment in these sectors, besides providing a road map for exploiting the opportunities available for further investments. State Credit seminars are convened by Regional offices of NABARD annually where all agencies concerned, viz., the State Governments, Banks, NGOs, etc., participate and discuss policies and operational measures required for tackling constraints in development of the potential available in agriculture and allied sectors in the State. These seminars are aimed at action planning by all concerned to promote development through credit and non-credit support services. Under National level function, NABARD facilitates Government of India, RBI and State Governments in undertaking policy decisions regarding credit flow to agriculture and rural development.

3.4 Credit Products and Clients

3.4.1 Short-term Credit: In order to ensure availability of timely credit to farmers, banks follow production-oriented system of lending covering various agricultural operations based on area under different crops and crop-wise scales of finance. Refinance is provided by way of credit limits for financing such agricultural operations at concession rates of interest to State Cooperative Banks (SCBs), District Central Co-operative Banks (DCCBs) and Regional Rural Banks (RRBs). In addition to improving the flow of marketing credit to cultivators for augmenting their produce-holding capacity and checking incidence of distress sale, NABARD encourages the co-operative banks and Regional Rural Banks to finance marketing of crops, through its refinance facility for the purpose.

NABARD has ensured timely supply of agri-inputs like fertilizers, pesticides, etc., a line of credit is made available to Cooperative Banks for financing apex/Primary Societies for stocking and distribution of agricultural inputs. Refinance is provided to Cooperative Banks for financing production and marketing activities of industrial cooperative societies engaged in one or more of the 22 approved broad groups of cottage and small scale Industries (SSIs). Considering the importance of handloom sector in rural employment generation, refinance is extended to SCBs/CBs to meet the working capital requirements of primary/Apex Weavers' societies and State Handloom Development Corporations (SHDCs).

The High Level Committee appointed by Ministry of Textiles (MOT), Government of India, to suggest measures for revival of handloom sector has recommended organizing weavers outside the cooperative fold/members of non-viable or defunct Primary Weavers' Cooperative Societies (PWCSs)/weavers in areas of weak cooperative credit structure into Handloom Weavers Groups (HWGs) on the lines of Joint Liability Groups (JLGs) focusing on handloom clusters. A scheme formulated by NABARD envisages financing the production/investment/consumption needs of the members of HWGs by the Commercial Banks, Cooperative Banks and Regional Rural Banks. Refinance is provided to State Cooperative Banks and Commercial Banks for financing State Handicraft Development Corporation for production, procurement and marketing of handicrafts. Refinance facility is extended to Cooperative Banks and Regional Rural Banks for meeting the short term working capital requirements of farmers engaged in pisiculture activities.

3.4.2 Medium Term Credit: Refinance by way of medium term loans is granted to Cooperative Banks and Regional Rural Banks to enable them to convert the short term loans into medium term loans in respect of farmers, whose repayment capacity is affected due to substantial crop loss, as declared by the State Government, on account of natural calamities. The repayment period of the converted loan is 3 years, which may be extended to a maximum of 7 years in case of recurring calamities. Refinance is provided to State Cooperative Banks and Regional Rural Banks for financing farmers to acquire productive assets for certain approved agriculture investment purposes.

3.4.3 Investment Credit: Investment credit leads to capital formation through asset creation. It induces technological up gradation resulting in increased production, productivity and incremental income to farmers and entrepreneurs. NABARD provides refinance support to State Cooperative Agriculture and Rural Development Banks, State Cooperative Banks, Regional Rural Banks, CBs, Scheduled primary Urban Cooperative Banks, North East Development Finance Corporation Ltd. (NEDFI), etc., against their investment credit in rural sector. Major purposes covered are farm mechanization, minor irrigation, plantation/horticulture, animal husbandry, storage/market yards, fisheries, post harvest management, food/agro processing, non-farm sector including rural industries, micro finance, purchase of land (for small/marginal farmers, share croppers, etc.), rural housing and disbursements under poverty alleviation programs like SGSY, SC/ST action plan etc. Hi-tech projects and agri-export zones are identified as thrust areas. NABARD also helps the client institutions in techno-economic appraisal of projects besides providing refinance. The technical feasibility of the project, financial viability and incremental income generation to the ultimate borrowers, thereby enabling them to have a reasonable surplus after repayment of the loan installments are the necessary conditions to be satisfied for sanctioning refinance for investment credit. The period of loan ranges between 3 and 15 years depending on the purpose for which it is provided.

3.4.4 Direct Credit: In order to strengthen the owned funds position of cooperative credit institutions and thereby increasing their capacity to leverage larger resources, NABARD provides loans to the State Governments to contribute to the share capital of these institutions. With the objective of assisting the State Governments in completion of ongoing rural infrastructure projects, the Rural Infrastructure Development Fund (RIDF) was setup by with NABARD in 1995-96 with contributions from commercial banks by way of deposits. The cumulative allocation covering RIDF - I (1995-96) to XII (2006-07) is Rs.60,000 crore (excluding amount sanctioned under a separate window for *Bharat Nirman*). The sanction under each tranche has a phasing of 2-3 years. Sanctions under all the tranches of RIDF as on 31st March, 2007 stood at Rs. 61539.87 crore against which the disbursements stood of Rs. 37559.92 crore. The allocation to RIDF XIII has been enhanced and fixed at Rs.12000 crore during 2007-08.

3.4.5 Co-finance: NABARD has entered into agreements with 15 Commercial Banks for co-financing hi-tech/export oriented agriculture projects involving large financial outlays/sunrise technologies, etc., thereby sharing the credit risks with partner banks. NABARD has decided to participate in co-financing arrangement with Regional Rural Banks and Cooperate Banks also on a highly selective basis and with other institutions, viz., NAFED, NCDC, NDDB, etc., if a scheduled bank is involved in the arrangement. NABARD had been selectively extending Revolving Fund Assistance to Micro Finance Institutions for lending to Self-help Groups. During the year, Rs.100 lakh has been sanctioned taking the aggregate RFA to Rs. 27.32 crore to 31 agencies.

3.4.6 Automatic Refinance: Refinance is available under Automatic Refinance Facility (ARF) subject to ceiling of Rs.15 lakh for a new unit and Rs. 5 lakh for renovation/repairs per housing unit in case of Commercial Banks/Regional Rural Banks/Scheduled Urban Cooperative Banks and NEDIF. Financing Banks need to obtain prior sanction in respect of group proposals. Refinance would be 90 per cent of the bank loan. The quantum of refinance would be 100 per cent for State Cooperative Agriculture and Rural Development Banks, District Rural Industries Project districts and Norht Eastern Region including Sikkim.

3.4.7 Interest Rates on Refinance Assistance: The rates of interest on ST/MT refinance to co-operative banks, Regional Rural Banks and scheduled commercial banks and long-term (LT) loans to State Government for contribution to share capital of co-operative credit institutions during 2006-07 have been indicated in Table 3.1.

Table 3.1: Rates of Interest

(Per cent)

Sr. No.	Purpose	Agency	Interest Rate
1.	SAO	SCBs/RRBs	2.5/4.5
2.	Pledge of Securities	SCBs	8.5
3.	Working capital requirements of pisciculture/fishery activities	SCBs & RRBs	8.25
4.	Marketing of crops	SCBs & RRBs	8
5.	Collection and Marketing of minor forest produce	SCBs	8.25P-8.5A
6.	Production/Procurement and marketing of cloth by WCS	SCBs	6P-6.25A
7.	Procurement and supply of yarn by Apex/ Regional WCS	SCBs	6.25
8.	Working capital requirements of SHDCs & SHnDCs	SCBs & Schedule	8.5
9.	Industrial Co-operative Societies (other than WCS)	Commercial Banks	6P-6.25A
10.	Rural artisans, including Weaver members of PACS/LAMPS/FSS	SCBs	6
11.	Procurement, stoking and distribution of fertilizers and other agricultural inputs	SCBs	8.25@- 8.50@@
12.	Working capital requirements of co-operative sugar factories against repledge of sugar stock	SCBs	
13.	ST-OSAO loans		11
14.	Financing of PWCS	SCBs, RRBs	8
15.	ST approved agricultural, allied and marketing activities	Schedule Commercial	6
16.	MT (non-schematic) loans	Bank	8.5
17.	MT- financing purchase of shares in co-operative processing societies	SCBs	8/8.5
18.	LT loans to State Governments	SCBs/RRBs	
19.	Conversion of ST loans into MT loans in areas affected by natural calamities	SCBs	8
20.	MT (conversion) loan	State Governments	8
21.	Liquidity support	SCBs	2.5
		RRBs	4.5
		SCBs & RRBs	8.5

A: Apex Societies. P: Primary Societies. @: Retail distribution of fertilizers. @@: Wholesale distribution of fertilizers.

As per the announcement in Union Budget 2006-07, to

make available ground level credit at 7 per cent to farmers availing crop loan up to Rs. 3 lakh for kharif 2006 and rabi 2006-07, NABARD extended refinance to co-operative banks and Regional Rural Banks at 2.5 and 4.5 per cent p.a., respectively, with interest subvention from Government of India. The refinance was made available to those SCBs and Regional Rural Banks, which together with their own involvement, provided crop loans at 7 per cent p.a. to farmers. Further, Government of India made available through NABARD, a subvention of 2 per cent p.a. to co-operative banks for ST credit disbursed up to Rs. 3 lakh per borrower during 2006-07 out of their own resources subject to banks providing such credit to farmers at 7 per cent p.a.

3.4.8 Eligibility Criteria for Refinance Assistance: The norms of getting refinance by various agencies under schematic lending for 2006-07 were revised. Gross/net non performing assets or recovery to demand, net worth and profitability formed the basis for classifying banks into A and B categories. Co-operative banks and Regional Rural Banks that did not fall under either category were required to prepare rehabilitation/business development plan for availing refinance from NABARD.

Though the quantum of refinance for co-operative banks and Regional Rural Banks was linked to risk perceptions, State Cooperative Banks/State Cooperative Agriculture and Rural Development Banks were entitled for additional refinance to the extent of 10 per cent of their core eligibility on initiating reform measures. However, banks with perceptible improvement in gross/net NPA position (as on 31 March 2006) or recoveries (as on 30 June 2006), improved lending, deposit mobilization, diversification of loan portfolio and improved internal control system, were eligible for higher quantum of refinance. Refinance support for Micro-finance under the SHG-Bank linkage programme was extended without reckoning it towards the quantum of eligibility.

3.5 Sources of Funds

3.5.1 Capital: The authorized capital of NABARD continued to be Rs. 5,000 crore as also the paid up capital which remained the same since 2001-2002 at Rs. 2,000 crore (Rs. 550 crore subscribed by the Government of India and Rs.1,450 crore by the RBI) as on 31 march 2007. The sources and uses funds of NABARD are given in Table 3.2.

Table 3.2: Statement of Sources and Uses of Funds

(Rs. crore)

Sources of funds	As on March 2007	Uses of Funds	As on March 2007
Capital	2,000	Cash & Bank balance	7,011
Reserves & Surplus	7,802	Investments	1,438
NRC(LTO) fund	13,214	a) GoI Securities	1,438
NRC(Stabilization) fund	1,533	b) ADFC Equity	16
Deposit	82	c) AFC Equity	1
Bonds & Debentures	28,892	d) SIDBI Equity	48
Borrowings from GoI	382	e) AICI Ltd	60
Borrowings from RBI	0	f) NCDEX Ltd & MCX Ltd	6
Borrowings from Commercial Banks	2,500	g) Nabcons	5
Foreign Currency Loan	289	h) Mutual Fund	500
RIDF Deposit	20,155	i) BVF APIDC V Investment	3
Other Liabilities	2,364	j) CBLO	304
Other Funds	2,007	k)Bills Rediscounted	0
		Loans & advances	
		a) Production & marketing Credit	14,758
		b) Conversion	181
		c) Liquidity Support	2,491
		d) MT Investment Credit (Non Project)	1
		e) MT & LT Project Loans	31,683
		f) LT Non Project Loan	335
		g) Others Loans	13
		h) RIDF Loans	20,005
		i) Co Finance	42
		Fixed Assets	238
		Others Assets	2,081
Total	81,220	Total	81,220

Source: NABARD, Annual Report, *2006-07*

3.5.2 Deposits: Deposits from tea, coffee and rubber companies outstanding as on 31st March, 2007 aggregated Rs. 81.38 crore. The deposits from Government of India under the Special Loan Account for financing ineligible farmers under the Command Area Development Programme were repaid during the year. Similar deposits from State Governments outstanding under the programme amounted to Rs.77 lakh as on 31st March, 2007.

During the year, NABARD received deposits from commercial banks aggregating Rs. 6,966.43 crore under RIDF V to XII. Repayments of Rs.786.10 crore were made to commercial banks under RIDF VI to IX up to 31st March, 2007. Deposits outstanding under various tranches of RIDF as on 31st March, 2007 were Rs. 20,154.70 crore as against Rs. 13,974.37 crore as on 31st March, 2006.

3.5.3 Bonds: Government of India has withdrawn the option available to NABARD for raising resources through issue of Capital Gains Bonds (CGBs), Tax Free Bonds and Priority Sector Bonds (PSBs) with effect from 1 April 2006. Consequently, the issue of Corporate Bonds became a major source of raising resources during 2006-07. During the year, NABARD obtained approval for raising resources by way of floating Bhavishya Nirman Bonds (Zero Coupon Bonds), through which an amount of Rs. 3.99 crore was raised.

3.5.4 Funds from Government of India: During the year, an account of Rs 17.83 crore was repaid on maturity to Government of India against the loans drawn earlier under various externally aided projects.

3.5.5 Borrowings under the General Line of Credit (GLC) from RBI: NABARD has been providing ST refinance to SCBs/RRBs for various purposes as per provisions of Section 21 of the NABARD Act, 1981, out of the GLC sanctioned to it every year by RBI. The activities covered under such refinance included ST-SAO, other non-agricultural purposes, financing to weavers' co-operatives, etc. RBI had sanctioned an aggregate GLC limit of Rs. 3,000 crore for the period April 2006 to January 2007. The entire outstanding amount was repaid to RBI on 31st January, 2007.

3.6 Uses of Funds

3.6.1 Schematic Lending: The amount outstanding under schematic lending, including subscriptions to Special Development Debentures of SCARDBs, was Rs. 31,682.46 crore as on 31st March, 2007 as against Rs. 30,157.41 crore as on 31st March, 2006.

3.6.2 Short-term, Medium-term and Medium-term (Conversion) Loan Assistance: The ST loans advanced for financing SAO to the SCBs (Rs. 11, 508.89 crore) and RRBs (Rs. 2,778.31 crore) together with loans under NABARD Line of Credit to SCBs (Rs. 106.90 crore) and other ST loans to SCBs (Rs. 196.61 crore) and RRBs (Rs. 166.85 crore) increased to Rs. 14, 757.56 crore as on 31st March, 2007 from Rs. 9,617.35 crore as on 31st March, 2006. The amount outstanding under MT investment non-project loans as on 31st March, 2007 stood at Rs. 0.19 crore. The amount outstanding under MT (conversion) loans as on 31st March, 2007 stood at Rs. 181.48 crore compared to Rs. 267.02 crore as on 31st March, 2006. The amount outstanding under the Liquidity Support Scheme for SCBs and RRBs aggregated Rs. 2, 490.60 crore as on 31st March, 2007 as against Rs. 2,491.80 crore as on 31st March, 2006.

3.6.3 Loans to State Governments

A. Project Loans under RIDF: The project loans to state governments under RIDF stood at Rs. 20,004.83 crore as on 31st March, 2007, compared to Rs. 15,142.41 crore as on 31st March, 2006.

B. Non-project Loans: The amount outstanding under the non- project LT loans to state governments for contribution to the share capital of co-operative credit institutions, amounted to Rs. 335.14 crore as on 31st March, 2007, compared to Rs. 387.49 crore as on 31st March, 2006.

C. Other Loans: Other loans outstanding stood at Rs.

13.20 crore as on 31st March, 2007, which included amounts outstanding under various funds, viz. CDF, MFDEF, and WDF.

3.6.4 Investment of Surplus Funds: NABARD deployed its ST surplus funds in ST deposits with commercial banks. During the year, NABARD liquidated its ST deposits and G-sec investment to support its business operation. As on 31st March, 2007, the total investments of the surplus funds of the bank in ST deposits, money market instruments, government securities etc., aggregated Rs. 9, 203.14 crore.

3.6.5 Co–finance: The Bank has entered into agreements with commercial banks to co-finance various projects. The outstanding as on 31st March, 2007 aggregated Rs. 42.43 crore.

3.7 Organisation and Management

NABARD attaches great importance to the capacity building of its employees and the up gradation of their skill and technical expertise. To this end, the Bank continued to refine its existing training modules, introduced new programmes and enhanced the exposure of its staff through visits to various institutions within the country and abroad.

3.7.1 Board of Directors: The Board of Directors met five times during the years. The Executive Committee, the Sanctioning Committee for loans under RIDF and the Audit Committee of Board met six, seven and four times, respectively. The Risk Management Committee of Board met thrice during the year.

3.7.2 Inspection of NABARD: Reserve Bank of India conducted the ninth round of financial inspection of NABARD from 20th November, 2006 to 17th January, 2007, with refinance to the financial position as on 31st March, 2006.

3.7.3 Regional/District Development Managers Offices: Besides the corporate office at Mumbai, NABARD has 28 ROs, sub-office at Port Blair, a cell at Srinagar and training establishments at Bolpur, Hyderabad, Lucknow and

Mangalore. District Development Manager (DDM) offices have been functioning in 391 of the 597 districts in the country, of which 15 DDM offices were opened during the year. In addition, 88 districts are tagged to these DDM offices.

3.7.4 Staff Strength: The total staff strength of the Bank stood at 5,045 as on 31st March, 2007, of which 1,290 belong to SC (17.4 per cent) and ST (8.2 per cent) categories. The staff strength of ex-serviceman and physically handicapped employees stood at 107 and 104 constituting 2.1 and 2 per cent, respectively, of the total staff strength.

3.8 Welfare Measures for SC/ST Employees

The Bank adhered to instructions issued by Government of India from time to time regarding reservations for SCs/STs through direct recruitment as also through promotions in all grades up to which the Bank has accepted to provide reservations. Quarterly meetings by Senior Executives and the Chief Liaison Officer with representatives of the Welfare Association of SC/ST were held regularly at HO and Regional Offices. Other benefits extended to these employees included, (i) conduct of pre-promotional training programmes for 80 officers and 37 employees in Group 'B' and (ii) disbursement of an amount of Rs. 2.37 lakh awarded to 77 wards of SC/ST employees under the scholarship and book grant schemes.

Housing loans aggregating Rs. 2,368.26 lakh were sanctioned to 380 employees during the year. The disbursements against sanctions, including loans sanctioned in previous year, amounted to Rs. 2,058.77 lakh.

3.9 Overseas Training/Exposure Visits

The officers were deputed for various overseas training programmes, exposure visits and seminars. Among these were faculty members from various training establishments of the Bank who were deputed for a Faculty Development Programme at the Centre for International Development and Training, Wolver Hampton University, UK. Other institutions associated with the visits/programmes were International Institute of Rural Reconstruction (IIRR), Philippines; APRACA-CENTRAB, CICTAB, GTZ-KfW, Germany and Weitz Centre for Development Studies, Israel. Officers from Nabcons visited Kenya for undertaking consultancy assignments.

3.10 Industrial Relations

Harmonious industrial relations were restored with the signing of a settlement on wage revision and service conditions of the employees between the Bank and All India NABARD Employee' Association on 11th August, 2006. The Memorandum of Settlement, effective from 1st November, 2002 for a period of five years was arrived at on the basis of well established principles of negotiation, mutual trust and respect, resulting in effective and efficient manpower utilization by the Bank. The pay and allowances and service conditions of officers of the Bank were also revised after arriving at an undertaking with the National Bank Officers' Association. The Central Complaints Committee at HO and the 22 Regional Complaints Committees at Regional Offices are functioning for prevention of sexual harassment of women at the work place.

3.11 Data Management

The erstwhile Department of Information Systems and Computer services (DISCS) was restructured and christened as the Central Statistical Information Department (CSID). The mandate of CSID was enlarged to include collection and processing of data from various sources and dissemination of information related to agricultural and rural sector to various agencies, provide technical guidance related to data management and data warehousing within the Bank and publish statistical reports and hand books periodically. During 2006-07, CSID prepared a statistical profile of NABARD that included business related information since inception of the

Bank, a district level database covering parameters, viz. physical-geographical features, workers profile, land holding, agriculture infrastructure, etc. and reviewed the existing system of data collection in major HO departments so as to rationalize the returns.

3.12 Information Technology

NABARD introduced corporate e-mail solution in the Bank. The 'NABARD mail' has been made operational at HO, 19 Regional Offices and all district level officers and has been found to be very effective and user friendly. The remaining Regional Offices will be brought into the fold of corporate e-mail solutions shortly.

3.13 Public Relations

NABARD has taken various initiatives to disseminate its schemes, programmes, expectations, innovations and achievements with various agencies as well as to the general public. Among the important events organized during the year were exhibitions of products at Ahmedabad, Chandigarh, Meghalaya, Mumbai (Saras Handicrafts Mela) and Sunderban. A phone-in question and answer radio programme on various issues of agriculture and rural development was introduced for the general public in Jharkhand and in the States of NER. Besides, the Bank continued to publish its quarterly and monthly publications-NABARD Parivar and NABARD Newsletter, respectively. A campaign was also launched to promote the Rural Innovation Fund (RIF) through print media and for the Zero Coupon Bonds called 'Bhavishya Nirman Bonds' launched with effect from 1st February, 2007 to attract small savings from the general public to pool them into a fund to be utilized for various activities connected with agriculture and rural development.

3.14 Visit of Parliamentary Committees

Eleven Parliamentary Committees held discussions with

NABARD on various aspect concerning rural credit delivery, rural development, women empowerment, DFI status of NABARD, etc. These were, (i) Committee on Examination of Demands for Grants (2006-07) on Agriculture-Evidence of representatives of DAC, (ii) Department related Committee on Personnel, Public Grievances, Law and Justice, (iii) Committee on Finance in connection with the examination of Funding of SHGs (iv) Department related Committee on Industry, (v) Sub-Committee on Drafting and Evidence of Parliament on Drafting and Evidence of Parliament on Official Language Implementation, (vi) Study Tour of Standing Committee on Finance, (vii) On the spot study visit by the Committee on Agriculture, (viii) Committee on Food, Consumer Affairs and Public Distribution, (ix) Study Tour by the Committee on Petitions, (x) Study Tour by the Committee on Empowerment of Women and (xi) Committee on Government Assurances.

4

Refinancing Schemes of NABARD

The refinance facilities are provided by NABARD to financial institutions namely State Cooperative Agriculture and Rural Development Banks (SCARDBs), Commercial Banks (CBs), State Cooperative Banks (SCBs), Regional Rural Banks (RRBs), and Agricultural Development Finance Companies/Primary Urban Cooperative Banks (ADFCs/PUCBs), which supply credit for agricultural and rural development. The refinance facility is spread over fifteen schemes namely refinance for minor irrigation, land development, farm mechanisation, plantation and horticulture, poultry farm, sheep, goat and piggery farming, fisheries, dairy development, forestry, storage and market yards, Integrated Development Programme (IRDP), non-farm sector, Swarnajayanti Gram Swarozgar Yojana (SGSY), SC/ST Action plan, self-help groups, bio-gas scheme and others including financial assistance for bullock carts, etc. The features of each of the schemes are presented below.

4.1 Minor Irrigation Scheme

Irrigation is the most important input for of agricultural development. Water is very much essential for plant growth. When adequate quantity of water is not available to the plant either due to low rainfall or uneven distribution during the cropping season, additional dose of water is usually provided for optimum plant growth, lest the plant dies out of water hunger. Thus, artificial application of water in the field to maintain optimum soil moisture is called irrigation. India is endowed with good amount of rainfall (1194 mm) but due to inefficient management, large amount of rainwater flows down as run off. So far, the total area under irrigation is only 36 per cent (gross irrigated area).

Hence, there is a good scope for storing the rainwater by adopting different methods and recharging the ground for bringing more areas under irrigation. Irrigation projects have been classified into three categories according to their command area. In case of major, the command area in hectare is above 10000, medium 2000-10000 and minor command area in hectare is below 2000. Major and medium irrigation projects are however not refinanced by NABARD and are mostly undertaken by the Central and State Governments. The minor irrigation projects assist the farmers to get quicker benefits of irrigation. However, a proper mix of major, medium and minor projects could only lead to an efficient water source utilisation in a particular area. The main sources of water for irrigation are: surface water - e.g. dam, pond, tank, nullah, river etc; underground water - e.g. open well, bore, tube well etc.

4.1.1 Methods of Irrigation: The methods of irrigation classified into four categories namely flow irrigation, lift irrigation, manual irrigation, animal driven and mechanical. Through gravitational flow, water is led from dams, rivers, ponds to the fields in open channels and thus is called flow irrigation. Lift irrigation is water lifted from the surface/underground sources with the help of lifting devices. Manual device is water lifted through picottah/swing bucket. Water lifting through single or double mhote, Persian wheel is called animal driven, whereas when diesel or electronic pump set is used, it is called mechanical.

Normally, NABARD receives proposals for financing minor irrigation projects like open well, tube/bore well, river lift points, installation of pump sets and also for drip and sprinkler projects. The minor irrigation scheme involves three key activities namely tapping the water sources, lifting of water and the use of water for providing irrigation to crops. The irrigation systems are classified into macro irrigation and micro irrigation system. Macro irrigation system includes flood/bed/surge/furrow/gated pipe and basin whereas micro irrigation systems include drip and sprinkler irrigation.

It will be open to a beneficiary farmer to repay the loan amount earlier than the 11 months as prescribed period depending on his incremental income and ability.

4.1.2 Refinancing by NABARD for Minor Irrigation Scheme: The NABARD involvement in refinance for minor irrigation scheme is dealt below. Refinance disbursements throughout India and growth rate during 1982-83 to 2006-07 for minor irrigation scheme are furnished in Table 4.1.

Table 4.1: Disbursements for Minor Irrigation Scheme

Year	Disbursements (Rs. crore)		Share of M.I.S. Scheme (per cent)	YOY Rate
	M.I scheme	All scheme		
1982-83	244	703	34.70	-
1983-84	312	892	34.97	27.86
1984-85	335	1062	31.54	7.37
1985-86	517	1192	43.37	54.32
1986-87	483	1334	36.20	-6.57
1987-88	335	1482	22.40	-30.64
1988-89	387	1270	30.47	15.52
1989-90	498	1702	29.25	28.68
1990-91	496	1904	26.05	-0.40
1991-92	502	2054	24.44	1.20
1992-93	561	2359	23.78	11.75
1993-94	589	2745	21.45	4.99
1994-95	598	3011	19.86	1.52
1995-96	607	3063	19.81	1.50
1996-97	592	3523	16.80	-2.47
1997-98	524	3922	13.36	-11.48
1998-99	544	4521	12.03	3.81
1999-00	618	5215	11.85	13.60
2000-01	626	6158	10.16	1.29
2001-02	691	6682	10.34	10.38
2002-03	854	7418	11.51	23.58
2003-04	651	7605	8.56	-23.77
2004-05	680	8577	7.92	4.45
2005-06	541	8622	6.27	-20.44
2006-07	671	8795	7.62	24.02

Source: NABARD Annual Report (compiled and computed).

Table 4.1 reveals that the disbursement share of minor irrigation scheme to disbursement under all schemes operated by NABARD has risen over the years, except for few years. From a high of 27 per cent in 1983-84, the figure has fallen to 24.02 per cent in 2006-07. The main reason for this is the poor repayment performance of borrowers. With 31 per cent recovery, loan servicing is not satisfactory. The poor recovery is due to construction of wells not conforming to the recommended dimensions, unviable small size of the cultivated land holdings, low levels of output due to low fertilizer usage, etc. It must be, however, held in mind that the absolute allocation for minor irrigation schemes has risen from Rs. 244 crore in 1982-83 to Rs. 671 crore in 2006-07 recording a growth of about 175 per cent. However, the share of minor irrigation scheme on all schemes stood at 34.70 per cent during 1982-83 and at 7.62 per cent during 2006-07.

4.1.3 Agency-wise Refinance by NABARD: Agency-wise disbursement by NABARD throughout India under minor irrigation scheme up to the year ended 31st March 2007 is given in Table 4.2.

Table 4.2 Agency-wise Disbursement under Minor Irrigation Scheme

(Rs. crore)

Agency	Financial Assistance 2006-07	Commit -ment 2006-07	D during 2006-07	Share (%)	Cumulative D as on March 31, 2007	Share (%)
SCARDBs	180	171	171	25.6	9096	60.3
CBS	335	311	311	46.5	3635	24.1
SCBs	143	135	135	20.1	1667	11.0
RRBs	59	52	52	7.8	687	4.5
ADFCs/ PUCBs	-	-	-	-	0.49	0.1
Total	717	669	669	100	15085	100

D = Disbursement

Source: NABARD's Statistical Statement, (2006-2007)

4.2 Land Development Scheme

Judicious use of land and water resources, soil health

improvement and reclamation of degraded lands are prerequisites for increasing agricultural production. To promote sustainable agriculture, NABARD is making available refinance for this sector on priority. Financial help from banks can be availed of by individual farmers for measures like land levelling, terracing, bounding-contour bounding, graded bounding, bench retracting, contour trenching/stone walls/revetments/gully control measures, construction of farm ponds/nala bunds/check dams, construction of water ways, disposal drains, silt application, integrated measures etc. Rain-fed farming on watershed basis is identified as the key area of development needed for increasing food grain production and income in fragile ecosystems. NABARD gives top priority for this sector by giving hundred per cent refinance to implementing banks. Some of the investments for which bank finance is usually needed are:

- **Soil Conservation Works:** Contour bunds, graded bunds, graded border strips, bench terracing, zing terracing, grassed water ways, diversion drains, and vegetative measures.
- **Water Resource Development:** Farm ponds, nullah bunds/percolation tanks, stop/check dams.
- **Crop Production:** Improved agronomic packages, crop replacement/diversification, integrated pest management, organic manure production etc.
- **Water Management:** Under irrigation projects, poor water management and land development, results in water logging and land degradation leading to salinity. To prevent this, on farm development measures like land levelling and drainage channels are required. Credit schemes for this sub-sector can be drawn with tie-up for extension support. For efficient use of water under non command area development areas such as minor irrigation structures, lift irrigation schemes, bank finance can be availed for OFD works under automatic refinance facility

from NABARD.

- **Land Reclamation:** Unscientific and uncontrolled use of water in irrigation command areas has left productive lands uncultivated due to salinity and alkalinity. To bring back these degraded lands for higher productivity, NABARD gives refinance to banks for reclamation projects throughout the country.
- **Wasteland Development:** NABARD will approve any farm forestry scheme where the primary objective is to raise tree crops on wastelands for producing firewood, fodder, small timber and other non-timber forestry produce.

4.2.1 Disbursement by NABARD for Land Development Scheme: The annual disbursement of funds by NABARD for land development scheme at all India level for the period 1982-83 to 2006-07 is given in Table 4.3.

Table 4.3: Disbursement for Land Development Scheme

Year	Disbursements (Rs. crore)		Share of L.D Scheme (per cent)	YOY rate
	L.D scheme	All scheme		
1982-83	21	703	2.99	-
1983-84	29	892	3.25	38.10
1984-85	43	1062	4.05	48.28
1985-86	29	1192	2.43	-32.56
1986-87	52	1334	3.90	79.31
1987-88	21	1482	1.42	-59.62
1988-89	18	1270	1.42	-14.29
1989-90	11	1702	0.65	-38.89
1990-91	16	1904	0.84	45.45
1991-92	14	2054	0.68	-12.50
1992-93	13	2359	0.55	-7.14
1993-94	18	2745	0.66	38.46
1994-95	17	3011	0.56	-5.56
1995-96	29	3063	0.95	70.59
1996-97	44	3523	1.25	51.72
1997-98	59	3922	1.50	34.09
1998-99	64	4521	1.42	8.47
1999-00	75	5215	1.44	17.19

Contd...

2000-01	106	6158	1.72	41.33
2001-02	135	6682	2.02	27.36
2002-03	251	7418	3.38	85.93
2003-04	185	7605	2.43	-26.29
2004-05	291	8577	3.39	57.30
2005-06	637	8622	7.39	118.90
2006-07	651	8795	7.40	2.20

Source: NABARD Annual Reports (compiled and computed)

The disbursement share of Land Development Scheme compared to disbursement under all schemes operated by NABARD is not stable. The figure started from 2.99 per cent in 1982-83 and reached a mere 7.40 per cent during 2006-07. Because land development is highly technical and costly, most of the farmers do not like to get loan for this purpose. Moreover, in most cases, the cultivator refuses to accept the liability for loans as the work done is not to his satisfaction and the increase in yield is just marginal which leaves no surplus for repayment of the loan. Consequently, there are heavy arrears. The financing bank, viz., Land Development Bank was unwilling to grant loans to farmers due to poor recoveries. Hence, after the nineties, Special Loan Account (SLA) for land development purpose equally contributed by State Government and NABARD to farmers had been introduced. The disbursement share of land development scheme has been slightly increasing. From 0.95 per cent in 1995-96, the figure has gone up to 2.02 per cent in 2001-02. In this period, NABARD has conducted many land development programmes in various villages throughout India to create importance about land development and motivate the farmers to convert their uncultivable land into cultivable land. It must be, however, held in mind that the absolute allocation for Land Development Scheme has risen from Rs. 16 crore in 1990-91 to Rs. 135 Crore in 2001-02 recording a spectacular growth.

4.2.2 Agency-wise Disbursement under Land Development Scheme: Agency-wise disbursement by NABARD throughout India under Land Development Scheme for the year ended 31st March 2007 is given in Table 4.4.

Table 4.4: Agency-wise Disbursement under Land Development Scheme (Rs. crore)

Agency	Financial Assistance 2006-07	Commit ment 2006-07	D during 2006-07	Share (%)	Cumu- lative D as on March 31, 2007	Share (%)
SCARDBs	151	144	144	22.18	1302	45.10
CBs	481	458	458	70.57	1166	40.39
SCBs	36	33	33	5.08	234	8.10
RRBs	14	14	14	2.15	184	6.37
ADFC/ PUCBs	-	-	-	-	0.62	1.00
Total	682	649	649	100	2886.62	100

D = Disbursement

Source: Statistical Statement Issued by NABARD

4.3 Farm Mechanisation

Farm mechanisation means introduction of improved tools, implements, machines and management practices in agriculture and agro-processing to improve production, productivity, profitability and farm income and thereby ensuring a better rural living. At present, farmers are shifting from traditional methods to modern agriculture methods. Farm mechanisation is generally associated with the use of tractors, power tillers, harvester, combines and other machines used in agricultural operations. It also includes the use of improved tools like chaff cutter, thresher, seed and fertilizer drill, etc. The use of any mechanical device on farms, driven either by animal or human power is also considered farm mechanisation. The farm machines and mechanical devices may result in a direct increase in production or the cropping intensity. Increase in production results through rise in productivity caused by timely sowing, transplanting and deep ploughing facilitated by mechanisation using tractors or power tillers.

4.3.1 Technical Aspects of Refinance for Farm Mechanisation Devices: NABARD has been providing the refinance assistance for purchase of farm mechanical devices subject to: net area under cultivation, area under irrigation with source of irrigation, cropping pattern, topography of the land, its suitability for tractor use, availability of power sources, the list of farm implements and machinery - the farmer intends to purchase, particularly its make, model etc., farm implements and machinery already available with the farmer, availability of spare parts, after sale service, fuel and lubricants etc., number of existing tractors in the village to assess the scope for custom hiring and assessment of utilisation of the tractor in own farm and custom hiring.

4.3.2 Refinancing by NABARD for Farm Mechanization Scheme: The NABARD involvement in refinance for farm mechanization scheme is dealt below. The position of disbursement throughout India and growth rate during 25 years for farm mechanization scheme is furnished in Table 4.5. The financial disbursement under farm mechanization scheme on all schemes operated by NABARD has increased year over year from 20.91 per cent in 1982-83 to 32.69 per cent in 1999-2000.

Table 4.5: Disbursements for Farm Mechanization Scheme

Year	D (Rs. crore)		Share of F.M Scheme (%)	YOY rate
	F.M scheme	All scheme		
1982-83	147	703	20.91	
1983-84	204	892	22.87	38.78
1984-85	170	1062	16.01	-16.67
1985-86	205	1192	17.20	20.59
1986-87	151	1334	11.32	-26.34
1987-88	120	1482	8.10	-20.53
1988-89	158	1270	12.44	31.67
1989-90	225	1702	13.22	42.41
1990-91	338	1904	17.75	50.22
1991-92	381	2054	18.55	12.72
1992-93	518	2359	21.96	35.96
1993-94	631	2745	22.99	21.81
1994-95	685	3011	22.75	8.56
1995-96	701	3063	22.89	2.34

Contd...

1996-97	871	3523	24.72	24.25
1997-98	1099	3922	28.02	26.18
1998-99	1345	4521	29.75	22.38
1999-00	1705	5215	32.69	26.77
2000-01	1900	6158	30.85	11.44
2001-02	1359	6682	20.34	-28.47
2002-03	993	7418	13.39	-26.93
2003-04	827	7605	10.87	-16.72
2004-05	1055	8577	12.30	27.57
2005-06	1713	8622	19.87	62.37
2006-07	1857	8795	21.11	8.41

D = Disbursements

Source: NABARD Annual Reports (compiled and computed)

The increasing demand for refinance of tractor loans necessitated a review of NABARD's policy of further support to this development, in the context of the priority to be given for investments intended to benefit small and marginal farmers and for other diversified purposes. The overall recovery position of the loans saw a sharp decline and that the refinance disbursed for this purpose during the year 2006-07 declined.

4.3.3 Agency-wise Disbursement under Farm Mechanization Scheme: Agency-wise disbursement by NABARD throughout India under farm mechanization scheme up to/for the year ended 31st March 2007 is presented in Table 4.6.

The refinance assistance to the CBs /Co-operative Banks/ RRBs for their financing would be available under Automatic Refinance Facility i.e. without prior sanction of schemes.

4.4 Plantation and Horticulture

Plantation and horticulture broadly covers development of fruit crops like mango, grape, litchi, apple, guava, pomegranate, banana, citrus etc. and plantation crops like tea, coffee, coconut, rubber, oil palm, betel vine, etc. and condimental crops like rose, jasmine, gerbera, gladiolus, foliage plants etc. and spices like cardamom, pepper, clove, cinnamon, nutmeg etc., medicinal plants like guggul, pippali, aonla, isabgol, dioscorea, rauwolfia, pexiwinkle etc. and essential oil/aromatic plants like citronella, palmarosa, veltiver, mint etc and vegetable crops like parwal, kundru, squash etc and sericulture, apiculture, mushrooms, seed production and other related activities.

Table 4.6: Agency-wise Disbursement under Farm Mechanization Scheme

(Rs. crore)

Agency	Financial Assistance 2006-07	Commit-ment 2006-07	D during 2006-07	Share (%)	Cumulative D as on March 31, 2007	Share (%)
SCARDBs	334	302	302	16.28	8228	41.16
CBS	1531	1379	1379	74.34	8573	42.89
SCBs	107	96	96	5.17	1291	6.46
RRBs	90	78	78	4.20	1889	9.45
ADFCs/ PUCBs	-	-	-	-	8	0.04
Total	2062	1855	1855	100	19989	100

D = Disbursement

Source: Statistical Statement Issued by NABARD

The refinance support from NABARD to all the eligible financial institutions is available in respect of activities like new planting/replanting/intensive cultivation of plantation and horticulture crops. Rejuvenation of old orchards/ plantations, integrated horticulture development, mixed orchards, nursery development/tissue culture, bee-keeping, honey extraction, mulberry cultivation, cocoon rearing, drainage etc. Refinance is also available for post-harvest infrastructure facilities like pre-cooling, cold storage etc., processing units for fruits and vegetables, plantation crops, spices, medicinal and aromatic plants etc., infrastructure required for export oriented plantation and horticulture projects. Protected cultivation activities like greenhouse cultivation, etc., and mushroom cultivation and activities like production, processing, compost manufacture, spawn production etc. are also available for refinance from NABARD.

According to the Ministry of Food, the country wastes (average wastage 35 per cent), more fruits and vegetables than what U.K. consumes every year. Out of the total percentage of agro exports, fruits, vegetables, flowers and processed products contribute only 5.59 per cent. After the Green Revolution, Blue Revolution and the Yellow Revolution, we now have yet another revolution called the Rainbow Revolution. Horticultural crops cover 8 per cent of the net sown area (142.10 million ha). Focused attention to horticulture was given only during 8th Plan although the tune was set in the 7th Plan after achieving self sufficiency in food grains.

4.4.1 Techno-economic Aspects of Horticultural Crops: The varied agro-climatic conditions of the country provide us an excellent platform to emerge as a leading producer of horticultural crops. India is the second largest producer of fruits and vegetables after China. The total annual production of fruits (45.50 million tonnes) and vegetables (90.83 million tonnes) touched 136.33 million tonnes during 1999-2000, as against 87 million tonnes in 1991-92, thus recording a 64 per cent of growth in a period of 8 years. India's position in the international ranking in production of various fruits and vegetables as per the Indian horticulture database 2001 is as under: Apple (10), Banana (1), Mango (1), Papaya (2), Pineapple (4), Grapes (10), Total fruits (2); Brinjal (2), Cabbage (2), Cauliflower (1), Peas (1), Onion (2), Potato (3), and Total vegetables (2). Diversification and value addition will be the key words for Indian horticulture. However, there are many challenges like increasing irrigation facilities, improving productivity, qualitatively and quantitatively to be globally competitive, creating infrastructure for post harvest technology and giving priority to exports, which have to be met to make place ourselves globally competitive. There is a need to create proper facilities for value addition in horticultural crops. A tremendous boost was given to the development of horticulture sector during the 9th Plan allocation of Rs. 1,400 crore. In addition to various centrally sponsored schemes, a separate scheme for horticulture development through plastic-culture intervention was implemented aiming at production of protected cultivation through green house technology and increasing micro irrigation facilities through drip and sprinkler systems.

4.4.2 Disbursement of NABARD for Plantation and Horticulture Scheme: The position of disbursement throughout India and growth rate during last 25 years for plantation and horticulture scheme is furnished in Table 4.7.

Table 4.7: Disbursement for Plantation and Horticulture Scheme

Year	Disbursements (Rs. crore)		Share of P.H scheme (%)	YOY Rate
	P.H Scheme	All Scheme		
1982-83	27	703	3.84	-
1983-84	38	892	4.26	40.74
1984-85	47	1062	4.43	23.68
1985-86	99	1192	8.31	110.64
1986-87	110	1334	8.25	11.11
1987-88	48	1482	3.24	-56.36
1988-89	65	1270	5.12	35.42
1989-90	97	1702	5.70	49.23
1990-91	94	1904	4.94	-3.09
1991-92	99	2054	4.82	5.32
1992-93	105	2359	4.45	6.06
1993-94	122	2745	4.44	16.19
1994-95	129	3011	4.28	5.74
1995-96	138	3063	4.51	6.98
1996-97	149	3523	4.23	7.97
1997-98	186	3922	4.74	24.83
1998-99	182	4521	4.03	-2.15
1999-00	195	5215	3.74	7.14
2000-01	247	6158	4.01	26.67
2001-02	280	6682	4.19	13.36
2002-03	292	7418	3.94	4.29
2003-04	251	7605	3.30	-14.04
2004-05	236	8577	2.75	-5.98
2005-06	322	8622	3.73	36.44
2006-07	314	8795	3.57	-2.48

Source: NABARD Annual Reports (complied and computed)

The disbursement share of plantation and horticulture scheme compared to disbursement under all schemes operated by NABARD has increased year by year. Since 1982-83, with Rs. 27 crore as disbursement, it rose to Rs. 314 crore in 2006-07, recording a growth rate of 1063 per cent. However, the share of allocation to plantation and horticulture sector was still about 3.57 per cent only.

4.4.3 Agency-wise Refinance by NABARD: Agency-wise disbursement by NABARD throughout India under Plantation and horticulture scheme is given in Table 4.8.

Table 4.8: Agency-wise Disbursement under Plantation and Horticulture Scheme

(Rs. crore)

Agency	Financial Assistance 2006-07	Commit-ment 2006-07	D during 2006-07	Share (%)	Cumulative D as on March 31, 2007	Share (%)
SCARDBS	156	144	144	46.15	2215	56.25
CBS	145	124	124	39.74	1110	28.19
SCBs	39	34	34	10.89	500	12.70
RRBs	12	10	10	3.20	110	2.79
ADFC/PUCBs	-	-	-	-	3	0.08
Total	352	312	312	100	3938	100

D = Disbursement

Source: NABARD's Statistical Statement (2006-2007)

4.5 Dairy Farming

The importance of dairy in the Indian economy can be gauged from the fact that the milk is the single largest commodity whose estimated value is Rs 500 billion, way ahead of the contribution made by rice and wheat. The estimated value of the milch animals alone is around Rs. 370 billion. Bovines provide 52 million H.P. equivalent to renewable source of energy through 84 million draught animals. Dairy animals also contribute to hides/skin and dung valued at Rs. 64 billion. Dairy sector provides additional income and generates job opportunities for 80 million farmer families. More than 70 per cent of marginal farmers and landless labourers maintain dairy animals to supplement their income. Women contribute 71 per cent of the force to dairy as compared with their share 33 per cent in crop farming. At present, India stands number one in total milk production in the world.

The annual output of dairy industry is Rs 1,08,000 crore. Production of milk rose from 20.7 million tonnes during the year 1969-70 to 84 million tonnes during 2001-02. The organized sector handles only 15 per cent, 40 per cent is retained by rural producers, while 45 per cent is still handled by traditional sector. Out of 15 per cent handled by the organized sector, only 50 per cent of it i.e., 7.5 per cent of the total milk production is handled in private sector. In India, 52 per cent of the milk is produced by buffaloes, 45 per cent by cows and only 3 per cent of the milk is contributed by other species namely goat, sheep etc., India has the largest bovine population in the world i.e. 19.2 per cent. Operation Flood has played a wonderful role in the development of dairying in India. Now, we have more than 1,03,000 milk Co-operative Societies in India in 264 districts as per AMUL pattern. Dairy in India is at present growing at the rate of 6.5 per cent per annum.

The following factors are taken into consideration by NABARD before refinancing for dairy purpose: the successful events of dairy farming in the past in the area and any adverse feature noticed in the past. The climate for raising dairy cattle; minimum grazing area required for cattle; availability of water supply (minimum clean drinking water requirement of cattle is about 130 to 150 litres/day) etc.

4.5.1 Refinancing by NABARD for Dairy Farming Scheme: The NABARD involvement in refinance in dairy development scheme is outlined below. The position of disbursement throughout India and growth rate during 1982-2007 for dairy development scheme is furnished in Table 4.9.

The disbursement share of dairy development scheme

compared to disbursement under all schemes operated by NABARD has increased year by year. The share rose from 3.41 per cent in 1982-83 to 5.73 per cent in 2006-07. The main beneficiaries of dairy programmes are small / marginal farmers and landless labourers.

Table 4.9 Refinancing by NABARD for Dairy Development Scheme

Year	Disbursements (Rs. crore)		Share of D.D scheme (%)	YOY Rate
	D.D Scheme	All scheme		
1982-83	24	703	3.41	0
1983-84	13	892	1.46	-45.83
1984-85	23	1062	2.17	76.92
1985-86	57	1192	4.78	147.83
1986-87	86	1334	6.45	50.88
1987-88	35	1482	2.36	-59.30
1988-89	51	1270	4.02	45.71
1989-90	75	1702	4.41	47.06
1990-91	73	1904	3.83	-2.67
1991-92	84	2054	4.09	15.07
1992-93	102	2359	4.32	21.43
1993-94	148	2745	5.39	45.10
1994-95	171	3011	5.68	15.54
1995-96	183	3063	5.97	7.02
1996-97	241	3523	6.84	31.69
1997-98	353	3922	9.00	46.47
1998-99	457	4521	10.11	29.46
1999-00	581	5215	11.14	27.13
2000-01	769	6158	12.49	32.36
2001-02	821	6682	12.29	6.76
2002-03	909	7418	12.25	10.72
2003-04	669	7605	8.80	-26.40
2004-05	754	8577	8.79	12.71
2005-06	695	8622	8.06	-7.82
2006-07	504	8795	5.73	-27.48

Source: NABARD's Statistical Statement (2006-2007)

A farmer can earn a gross surplus of about Rs. 12,000 per year from a unit consisting of 2 milking buffaloes. The capital investment required for purchase of 2 buffaloes is Rs. 18,223. Even after paying a sum of Rs. 4294 per annum towards repayment of the loan and interest, the farmer can earn a net surplus of Rs. 6000 to Rs. 9000 approximately per year. More profits can be earned depending upon the breed of animal, managerial skills and marketing potential. Moreover, the central and state governments are giving considerable financial assistance for creating infrastructure facilities for milk production.

4.5.2 Agency-wise Refinance by NABARD: Agency-wise disbursement by NABARD throughout India under Dairy Development scheme up to the year ended 31st March 2007 is given Table 4.10.

Table 4.10: Agency-wise Disbursement under Dairy Development Scheme

(Rs. crore)

Agency	Financial Assistance 2006-07	Commit-ment 2006-07	D during 2006-07	Share (%)	Cumulative D as on March 31, 2007	Share (%)
SCARDBs	256	231	231	45.83	5115	64.91
CBs	164	137	137	27.18	1073	13.61
SCBs	112	99	99	19.64	1272	16.14
RRBs	43	37	37	7.34	416	5.27
ADFC/PUCBs	-	-	-	-	4	0.05
TOTAL	575	504	504	100	7880	100

D = Disbursement

Source: NABARD's Statistical Statement (2006-2007)

4.6 Poultry, Sheep, Goat and Pigger Farming

Poultry meat and egg are important sources of high quality proteins, minerals and vitamins to balance the human diet. Specially developed breeds of chicken meat (broiler) and egg type chicken are now available with the ability of quick growth and high feed conversion efficiency. Depending on the farm size, layer (for eggs) farming can be a main source of family income or can provide subsidiary income and gainful employment to farmers throughout the year. Poultry manure has high fertilizer value and can be used for increasing the yield for all crops.

4.6.1 Scope for Layer farming and its National Importance: India has made considerable progress in egg production in the last three decades. High quality chicks, equipments, vaccines and medicines are available. Technically and professionally competent guidance is available to the farmers. The management practices have improved and disease and mortality incidents have reduced. Many institutions are providing training to entrepreneurs. The improved layer population has increased from 35 million in 1961 to 122 million in 1996. The egg production in the same period has increased from 2,340 million to 28600 million. The egg production registered a compound growth rate of 6.83 per cent during the Eighth Plan period (1992-97). The per capita egg availability at present is 33 eggs. Increasing assistance from the Central/State Governments and poultry corporations is being given to create infrastructural facilities so that new entrepreneurs can take up this business. Layer farming has been given considerable importance in the National Policy and has a good scope for further development.

NABARD is an apex institution for all matters relating to policy, planning and operations in the field of agricultural credit. It serves as an apex refinancing agency for the institutions providing investment and production credit. It promotes development through formulation and appraisal of project through a well organised Technical Service Department at the Head Office and Technical Cell at each of the Regional Offices.

Loan from banks with refinance facility from NABARD is available for starting poultry farming. The following technical aspects are considered before granting loan: for construction of brooder/grower and layer sheds, feed store, quarters etc.; for purchase of poultry equipment such as feeders, waterier and brooders etc.; for creating infrastructure items for supply of electricity, feed, water etc.; for purchase of one day old chicks or ready to lay pullets; for meeting working capital requirement in respect of feed, medicines and veterinary aid etc.

Sheep and goat farming is also an important aspect of this Farming. Sheep and goat farming contributes about 40 percent of the total meat requirement and provides employment to a large section of the weaker sections of the community in forest lands, hilly areas, agricultural waste land and pasture land.

Piggery is the most potential source of meat production and an efficient feed converter after the broiler. Apart from providing meat, it is also a source of bristles and manure. Pig farming provides employment opportunities to seasonally employed rural farmers and supplementary income to improve their living standards. The pig population in the country is 21.79 million as per the 2001 Livestock Census. The pork production stands at 6.20 tonnes (2001). During 2001-02, the value of pork and pork products were estimated to be Rs. 7.58 lakh. The contribution of pork products in terms of value works out to 0.80 per cent of total livestock products and 4.32 per cent of the meat and meat products. The contribution of pigs to Indian exports is very poor.

4.6.2 Refinancing by NABARD for Farming for P/S/G/P Scheme: The position of disbursement throughout India and growth rate during 1982 to 2007 for farming for P/S/G/P scheme are furnished in Table 4.11.

The disbursement share of farming for P/S/G/P scheme stood at 1.85 per cent in 1982-83. It rose to a peak of 5.39 per cent in 1995-96. After 1999-2000, refinance disbursement under this declined to 1.59 per cent of total disbursement by NABARD in 2006-07.

The main reason for the decline was that the commercial banks showed lesser interest in this class of finance keeping in view their liquidity position and the average cost of their resources.

It must be, however, held in mind that the absolute allocation for farming for P/S/G/P scheme has risen from Rs. 12 crore in 1990-91 to Rs. 106 crore in 2001-02, recording a growth of about 783 per cent. This is much higher than the growth rates in respect of all schemes during the above period, namely 251 per cent.

Table 4.11: Disbursement for Farming P/S/G/P Scheme

Year	Disbursements (Rs. crore)		Share of P/S/G/P Scheme (%)	YOY rate
	P/S/G/P Scheme	All scheme		
1982-83	13	703	1.85	-
1983-84	13	892	1.46	0
1984-85	23	1062	2.17	76.92
1985-86	46	1192	3.86	100.00
1986-87	54	1334	4.05	17.39
1987-88	22	1482	1.48	-59.26
1988-89	45	1270	3.54	104.55
1989-90	68	1702	4.00	51.11
1990-91	73	1904	3.83	7.35
1991-92	85	2054	4.14	16.44
1992-93	62	2359	2.63	-27.06
1993-94	96	2745	3.50	54.84
1994-95	140	3011	4.65	45.83
1995-96	165	3063	5.39	17.86
1996-97	184	3523	5.22	11.52
1997-98	199	3922	5.07	8.15
1998-99	227	4521	5.02	14.07
1999-00	218	5215	4.18	-3.96
2000-01	188	6158	3.05	-13.76
2001-02	176	6682	2.63	-6.38
2002-03	186	7418	2.51	5.68
2003-04	280	7605	3.68	50.54
2004-05	361	8577	4.21	28.93
2005-06	231	8622	2.68	-36.01
2006-07	140	8795	1.59	-39.39

Source: NABARD Annual Reports (complied and computed)

4.6.3 Agency-wise Refinance by NABARD: Agency-wise disbursement by NABARD throughout India under Poultry farming and farming for other animals (Goat, Sheep, Pig, etc.) up to the year ended 31st March 2007 is given in Table 4.12.

Table 4.12: Agency-wise Disbursement under Farming for P/S/G/P Scheme

(Rs. crore)

Agency	Financial Assistance 2006-07	Commit-ment 2006-07	D during 2006-07	Share (%)	Cumulative D as on March 31, 2007	Share (%)
SCARDBs	71	64	64	45.71	1997	66.04
CBs	35	29	29	20.71	764	25.26
SCBs	47	42	42	30.00	178	5.89
RRBs	98	5	5	3.57	78	2.58
ADFC/ PUCBs	-	-	-	-	7	0.23
Total	251	140	140	100	3024	100

D = Disbursement

Source: NABARD's Statistical Statement (2006-2007)

4.7 Fisheries Scheme

India with a total fish production of 560 million tonnes in 1998-99 occupies sixth position in the world and contributes a little over four per cent of the world fish production. Of the total fish produced, it is estimated that about 23 per cent is accounted by aquaculture and India ranks second in the world in aquaculture production contributing about 7 per cent of the total world production through aquaculture. The export earnings from marine products in 1999-2000 was to the tune of Rs. 5,096 crore which is more than nine times the exports made in 1987-88 of Rs. 531 crore. Export of marine products accounted for about 4 per cent of our Gross National Exports during 1999-2000. Fishery sector in India has been providing employment to about 59.60 lakh full time or part time fishermen. In addition another six million people are engaged in fishery related ancillary activities. The contribution of fishery sector to the Gross Domestic Product of the country is approximately 1.3 per cent.

The fisheries sector has grown at a steady pace of 6 per cent per annum during the 8th Five Year Plan. The sector can play an important role as a source of food security. During the period 1992-1996, the annual growth rate in food grain production fell from 6.6 per cent to 0.8 per cent. Thus, it is imperative that the increasing deficit in food supply can be supplemented with increasing production of marine products by utilizing other resources.

India has an estimated fish production potential of 8.4 million tonnes following conventional production technology. As against the said potential, the country is currently harnessing merely 5.6 million tonnes of fish. In view of the importance of the sector in the national economy, the NABARD has played a pivotal role in the development of the sector. The bank has so far provided refinance assistance to the tune of Rs. 61,321 lakh. All the activities subject to their techno-economic feasibility are covered under NABARD's refinance assistance

- **Marine Fisheries:** Marine fisheries are classified into capture and culture fisheries. Capture fisheries include traditional boats, motorisation of traditional crafts, mechanized fishing vessels and deep sea fishing. Culture fisheries include Mari culture in coastal waters and open sea culture in cages etc. During 2000-01, the value of exports of marine products aggregated to US$ 1,396 million as against US$ 1,1184 million during 1999-2000, recording an increase of 17.9 per cent.
- **Inland Fisheries:** Capture fisheries involve crafts/gears for fishing in reservoirs/rivers. On the other hand, culture fisheries comprises of composite fish culture, fish seed hatchery, culture of air breathing fishes, culture of trout, integrated fish culture, sewage fed fisheries, running water fish culture, ornamental fish breeding, fresh water prawn hatchery, monoculture/poly culture of freshwater prawn and fish and tilapia culture.
- **Brackish-Water Fisheries:** Brackish water fisheries includes shrimp farming in traditional/improved traditional/extensive/modified extensive system, shrimp hatchery and culture of other fin fishes like pearl oyster, edible oyster, mussels.

4.7.1 Refinance Disbursement by NABARD for Fisheries Scheme: The NABARD's involvement in refinance for fisheries schemes is outlined below. The position of disbursement at all India level and growth rate during the last 25 years for fisheries scheme is given in Table 4.13.

Table 4.13: Disbursement for Fisheries Schemes in India

Year	Disbursements (Rs. crore)		Share of Fisheries scheme (%)	YOY Rate
	Fisheries scheme	All Scheme		
1982-83	4	703	0.57	-
1983-84	7	892	0.78	75.00
1984-85	10	1062	0.94	42.86
1985-86	22	1192	1.85	120.00
1986-87	36	1334	2.70	63.64
1987-88	12	1482	0.81	-66.67
1988-89	19	1270	1.50	58.33
1989-90	21	1702	1.23	10.53
1990-91	21	1904	1.10	0.00
1991-92	31	2054	1.51	47.62
1992-93	31	2359	1.31	0.00
1993-94	55	2745	2.00	77.42
1994-95	101	3011	3.35	83.64
1995-96	107	3063	3.49	5.94
1996-97	41	3523	1.16	-61.68
1997-98	33	3922	0.84	-19.51
1998-99	30	4521	0.66	-9.09
1999-00	27	5215	0.52	-10.00
2000-01	34	6158	0.55	25.93
2001-02	36	6682	0.54	5.88
2002-03	35	7418	0.47	-2.78
2003-04	23	7605	0.30	-34.29
2004-05	26	8577	0.30	13.04
2005-06	38	8622	0.44	46.15
2006-07	38	8795	0.43	0.00

Source: NABARD Annual Reports (compiled and computed)

The share of disbursement to the fisheries sector was not constant. The steep rise in the disbursement of fisheries during 1994-95 and 1995-96 was mainly due to the spurt in development of brackish water fish farming in the country with technical assistance from abroad (Philippines, Taiwan and Japan). However, disbursement faced a downfall during the year 1996-97 due to the controversial issues raised against brackish water fish farming and public litigation filed in the Supreme Court which restricted the propagation of brackish water fish farming.

4.7.2 Agency-wise Refinance by NABARD: Agency-wise refinance by NABARD at all India level under fisheries scheme for the year ended March 31, 2007 is given in Table 4.14.

Table 4.14: Agency-wise Disbursement under Fisheries scheme

(Rs crore)

Agency	Financial Assistance 2006-07	Commit-ment 2006-07	D during 2006-07	Share (%)	Cumulative D as on March 31, 2007	Share (%)
SCARBs	5	5	5		337	38.75
CBs	22	18	18		412	47.37
SCBs	13	11	11		74	8.51
RRBs	5	4	4		46	5.29
ADFCs PUCBs	-	-	-	-	0.71	0.08
Total	45	38	38	100	869.76	100

D = Disbursement

Source: Statistical Statement Issued by NABARD (2006-2007)

Commercial banks have higher participation in financing fisheries and hence more than 47 per cent of NABARD refinance goes to them, followed by SCARBs (38 per cent), SCBs (8 per cent), RRBs (5 per cent) and ADFCs/PUCBs.

4.8 Storage and Market Yards Scheme

Nearly one-third of India's horticultural produce is wasted mainly on account of poor storage facilities. The Government of India appointed a High Level Expert Committee in November 1998 for improving the market condition and storage capacity for horticultural produce in the country. India has a very weak post-harvest storage and marketing infrastructure which causes a tremendous loss. A scheme for establishing cold storage and proper market place throughout the country with involvement of private enterprises for facilitating storage of horticultural produce is already in place and is being implemented by the Ministry of Agriculture with the help of NABARD. Besides providing business opportunities to cold storage owners, the facilities are used for cold storage of vegetables and their products, fresh fruits, dried fruits such as dates, raisins etc., and commodities other than horticultural produce in a separate chamber such as fish, egg, dairy products, etc.

A new capital investment subsidy scheme for construction/expansion/modernization of cold storage and market place for horticulture produce was introduced by the Government of India and implemented by National Horticulture Board (NHB), Ministry of Agriculture in collaboration with NABARD and National Co-operative Development Corporation (NCDC) at a cost of Rs. 175 crore during the period 1999-2000. The Scheme was a part of the on going Post Harvest Management (PHM) programme. The objectives of the Scheme is to create scientific storage capacity in rural areas to meet the requirements of farmers for storing farm produce; prevent distress sale of produce by farmers immediately after harvest; to promote pledge financing and marketing credit; and to introduce a national system of ware house in respect of agriculture commodities stored in such godowns, etc.

4.8.1 Refinance Disbursement by NABARD for Storage and Market Yard Scheme: The position of disbursement throughout India and growth rate during 1982 to 2007 for farming Storage and Market Yard scheme is given in Table 4.15.

The refinance disbursement under Storage and Market Yard Scheme generally has been very low. The share of refinance disbursement under this scheme compared to disbursement under all schemes operated by NABARD has hovered between 1.85 per cent and 0.41 per cent.

Table 4.15 Disbursement by NABARD for Storage and Market Yard Scheme

Year	Disbursements (Rs crore)		Share of S&M scheme (%)	YOY rate
	S&M scheme	All Scheme		
1982-83	13	703	1.85	-
1983-84	9	892	1.01	-30.77
1984-85	12	1062	1.13	33.33
1985-86	31	1192	2.60	158.33
1986-87	36	1334	2.70	16.13
1987-88	22	1482	1.48	-38.89
1988-89	16	1270	1.26	-27.27
1989-90	13	1702	0.76	-18.75
1990-91	14	1904	0.74	7.69
1991-92	9	2054	0.44	-35.71
1992-93	15	2359	0.64	66.67
1993-94	16	2745	0.58	6.67
1994-95	18	3011	0.60	12.50
1995-96	21	3063	0.69	16.67
1996-97	14	3523	0.40	-33.33
1997-98	14	3922	0.36	0.00
1998-99	16	4521	0.35	14.29
1999-00	15	5215	0.29	-6.25
2000-01	101	6158	1.64	573.33
2001-02	227	6682	3.40	124.75
2002-03	48	7418	0.65	-78.85
2003-04	25	7605	0.33	-47.92
2004-05	33	8577	0.38	32.00
2005-06	52	8622	0.60	57.58
2006-07	36	8795	0.41	-30.77

Source: NABARD Annual Reports (computed and compiled)

4.8.2 Agency-wise Refinance by NABARD: Agency-wise disbursement by NABARD throughout India under Storage and Market Yard scheme for the year ended 31st March 2007 is given in Table 4.16.

Table 4.16.Agency-Wise Disbursement under Storage and Market Yard Scheme

(Rs. crore)

Agency	Financial Assistance 2006-07	Commi-tment 2006-07	D during 2006-07	Share (%)	Cumulative D as on March 31, 2007	Share (%)
SCARDBs	77	69	69	63.89	165	17.48
CBs	30	27	25	23.15	619	65.57
SCBs	2	2	2	1.85	135	14.30
RRBs	1	12	12	11.11	24	2.54
ADFC/ PUCBs	-	-	-	-	1	0.10
TOTAL	110	110	108	100	944	100

D = Disbursement

Source: NABARD's Statistical Statement (2006-2007)

4.9 Forestry Scheme

In the context of the strategy to undertake massive need based and time bound programme in a forestation of wastelands, NABARD has liberalized its existing policy by extending refinance support to all bankable wasteland development programmes to make available credit through banking channels to the joint sector undertakings or private companies raising plantations for their raw material needs and for cooperatives or private entrepreneurs raising such plantations to meet raw material needs of such user industries with appropriate market tie up. Considering the national importance of this sector, NABARD is actively involved in the following activities. The total area of forests in India is 75.033 thousand hectares accounting for 22.97 per cent of total geographic area. The various state government owned forests amount to 94.89 per cent, communal forests 3.35 per cent and balance 1.76 per cent privately owned.

- **Farm Forestry:** Farm forestry involves the growing of trees on farmland along with agriculture or on bunds and boundaries of agricultural fields. The lands where farm forestry can be raised must be wastelands i.e., the lands which are lying barren and unutilized for many years. In other words, conversion of good agricultural land into mutually exclusive tree crops should be avoided.

- **Agro-forestry:** Growing of trees in combination with crops on agricultural lands. This is the only forestry practice approved by NABARD where good agricultural land can be used for forestry plantations along with agricultural crops. However, the number species of trees that can be raised on this land are very few viz, poplar, subabul, casuarina, kadam, eucalyptus, sissoo etc.
- **Commercial Forestry:** NABARD also provides refinance for raising forestry/farm forestry plantations by Forest Development Corporations/User Indutries/Wasteland Development Corporations etc. on Government wastelands, degraded forests and forest wastelands or private wastelands.
- **Commercial Nurseries:** NABARD provides refinance assistance for establishing nurseries on a small but viable scale with special emphasis on development of wastelands. The size of nursery may be such as will ordinarily be capable of producing a minimum of 30,000 seedlings thereby meeting the needs of 10 ha.wastelands.
- **Wasteland Development:** NABARD will approve any Farm Forestry scheme where the primary objective is to raise tree crops on wastelands for producing firewood, fodder, small timber and other Non-timer forestry produce.
- **Production Forestry:** This Programme is confined to reserved, protected and unclassified forests leased to forest corporations jointly owned by the Government of India and the respective State Government for development. The main purpose is the plantation of quick growing species with institutional finance in order to augment the supply of industrial wood. Under production forestry, the items of development are: i. nursery, ii. planting and maintenance, iii. salaries and wages iv. roads for transportation of labour and produce v. sailings for filed workers and labour vi. equipment etc. The cost of

development depends on the size of the program.

4.9.1 Refinance Disbursement by NABARD for Forestry Scheme: The NABARD involvement in refinance for forestry scheme is given below. The position of disbursement throughout India and growth rate during 25 years for forestry scheme is furnished in Table 4.17.

Table 4.17: Disbursement for Forestry Scheme

Year	Disbursements (Rs. crore)		Share of Forestry Scheme (%)	YOY rate
	Forestry scheme	All scheme		
1982-83	4	703	0.57	-
1983-84	5	892	0.56	25
1984-85	2	1062	0.19	-60
1985-86	20	1192	1.68	900
1986-87	25	1334	1.87	25
1987-88	6	1482	0.40	-76
1988-89	11	1270	0.87	83.33
1989-90	17	1702	1.00	54.55
1990-91	29	1904	1.52	70.59
1991-92	22	2054	1.07	-24.14
1992-93	25	2359	1.06	13.64
1993-94	20	2745	0.73	-20.00
1994-95	13	3011	0.43	-35.00
1995-96	11	3063	0.36	-15.38
1996-97	9	3523	0.26	-18.18
1997-98	11	3922	0.28	22.22
1998-99	9	4521	0.20	-18.18
1999-00	12	5215	0.23	33.33
2000-01	13	6158	0.21	8.33
2001-02	16	6682	0.24	23.08
2002-03	12	7418	0.16	-25.00
2003-04	11	7605	0.14	-8.33
2004-05	9	8577	0.10	-18.18
2005-06	7	8622	0.08	-22.22
2006-07	8	8795	0.09	14.29

Source: NABARD Annual Report 2006-2007 (compiled and computed)

The share of annual refinance disbursement under forestry scheme by NABARD to total disbursement of NABARD is not uniform. The figure has fallen to a mere 0.09 per cent in

2006-07. Even though NABARD is ready to provide sufficient refinance assistance, the borrowers are not ready to utilize the disbursed amount, because forestry development scheme is highly technical and the costliest one. Moreover, returns on investment accrues too late.

4.9.2 Agency-wise Refinance by NABARD: Agency–wise disbursement by NABARD throughout India under forestry scheme for the year ended 31st March 2007 is given in Table 4.18.

Table 4.18: Agency-wise Disbursement under Forestry Scheme

Agency	Financial Assistance 2006-07	Commit-ment 2006-07	D during 2006-07	Share (%)	Cumulative D as on March 31,2007	Share (%)
SCARDB	0.45	0.41	0.41	4.87	101	31.14
CBs	5	4	4	47.56	214	65.99
SCBs	4	4	4	47.56	4	1.23
RRBs	-	-	-	-	5	1.54
ADFCs/ PUCBs	-	-	-	-	0.29	0.09
Total	9.45	8.41	8.41	100	324.29	100

D = Disbursement

Source: Statistical Statement Issued by NABARD (2006-07)

4.10 Swarna Jayanthi Gram Swarozgar Yojana (SGSY)

Despite the efforts made by Government over the past few decades, rural poverty in India continues to be significant. Inspite of the poverty alleviation programmes initiated by the Government during successive years, the poverty levels in percentage terms has reduced from 56.44 per cent of India's population in 1973-74 to 26.10 per cent during 2000-2001. Although, there is a significant reduction in percentage terms, the absolute number of persons below poverty line as in March 2001 is quite large. Various poverty alleviation programmes implemented by Government over a period of time are Training of Rural Youth for Self-Employment, Development of Women and Children in Rural Areas, Supply of Improved Tools to Rural Artisans, Ganga Kalyan Yojana, Integrated Rural Development Programme and Million Wells Scheme.

The multiplicity of programmes being viewed as separate programmes in them resulted in lack of proper social intermediation, absence of desired linkages and the implementation being more concerned with achieving individual programme targets rather than focussing on the substantive issue of sustainable income generation. To rectify the situation, Government decided to restructure the self employment programme. A new programme namely "Swarna Jayanthi Gram Swarozgar Yojana"(SGSY) has been launched from April 1999. This is a holistic programme covering all aspects of self employment such as organisation of poor into Self Help Groups, Training, Technology, Infrastructure and Marketing. SGSY will be funded by the Central and State Governments in the ratio of 75:25. With the commencement of SGSY Scheme, all other earlier schemes mentioned above are no longer in operation with effect from 1.4.1999.

The main objective of SGSY will be to bring the assisted families (Swarojgaris) above poverty line in 3 years by providing them with income generating assets through a mix of bank credit and government subsidy. It would mean ensuring that the family will have a monthly net income of at least Rs. 2000 per month after meeting the loan repayment obligation. The effort will be to cover 30 per cent of the poor families every year in each block in a period of 5 years.

4.10.1 Salient Features of the Scheme: The salient features of the Scheme is the establishment of a large number of micro enterprises in rural areas, emphasis on group approach and group financing, to bring assisted families above poverty line in 3 years, holistic programme covering self employment, promoting Self-help Groups under group approach and financing, their capacity building, creation of activity clusters, infrastructure build up, training the beneficiaries, technology adoption, credit and marketing, cluster approach and activity clusters with 4-5 key activities for each block, adoption of project approach for group finance and identification of key activities, covering all families in five years period covering 30 per cent of poor families every year in the block, and identification of beneficiaries from Below Poverty Line (BPL) list through participatory process. It is a credit-cum-subsidy programme i.e. promotion of multiple credits to the same beneficiary to enable the beneficiary to cross poverty line within 3 years and skill development of "Swarojgaris" through training.

4.10.2 Refinancing by NABARD for SGSY Scheme: The NABARD involvement in refinance for SGSY scheme is dealt below. The position of disbursement throughout India and growth rate during the last 25 years for SGSY scheme are furnished in Table 4.19.

Table 4.19: Disbursements for SGSY Scheme

Year	Disbursements (Rs. Crore)		Share of SGSY (%)	YOY rate
	SGSY scheme	All scheme		
1982-83	185	703	26.32	-
1983-84	233	892	26.12	25.95
1984-85	354	1062	33.33	51.93
1985-86	383	1192	32.13	8.19
1986-87	338	1334	25.34	-11.75
1987-88	274	1482	18.49	-18.93
1988-89	403	1270	31.73	47.08
1989-90	549	1702	32.26	36.23
1990-91	602	1904	31.62	9.65
1991-92	647	2054	31.50	7.48
1992-93	649	2359	27.51	0.31
1993-94	662	2745	24.12	2.00
1994-95	620	3011	20.59	-6.34
1995-96	461	3063	15.05	-25.65
1996-97	513	3523	14.56	11.28
1997-98	611	3922	15.58	19.10
1998-99	735	4521	16.26	20.29
1999-00	590	5215	11.31	-19.73
2000-01	642	6158	10.43	8.81

Contd...

2001-02	559	6682	8.37	-12.93
2002-03	401	7418	5.41	-28.26
2003-04	229	7605	3.01	-42.89
2004-05	483	8577	5.63	110.92
2005-06	252	8622	2.92	-47.83
2006-07	355	8795	4.04	40.87

Source: NABARD Annual Reports (complied and computed)

The share of disbursement under SGSY scheme in the total disbursement made by NABARD in all schemes marginally increased from the year 1982-83 and reached the maximum of Rs. 8795 crore in 2006-07. Since the inception of the Program till 1998–99, 53.50 million families have been covered under SGSY at an expenditure of Rs. 13,700 crore. During the first two years of the Ninth Plan (1997-98 and 1998-99), about 3.37 million families are reported to have been covered of which 46 per cent were scheduled castes/scheduled tribes and 35 per cent were women. The total investment during this period has been Rs. 6,431 crore including a subsidy of Rs. 2,666 crore. After 1998-99, the disbursement position has been fluctuating.

4.10.3 Agency-wise Refinance by NABARD: Agency-wise disbursement by NABARD throughout India under SGSY scheme for the year ended 31st March 2007 is given in Table 4.20.

Table 4.20: Agency–wise Disbursement under SGSY Scheme

(Rs. crore)

Agencies	Financial assistance 2006-07	Commit-ment 2006-07	D during 2006-07	Share (%)	Cumulative D as on March 31, 2007	Share (%)
SCARDBs	1	1	1	0.28	270	2.24
CBs	257	257	257	72.60	5859	48.64
SCBs	11	11	11	3.11	1185	9.84
RRBs	96	85	85	24.01	4732	39.28
Total	365	354	354	100	12046	100

D = Disbursement

Source: NABARD Statistical Statement (2006-07)

4.11 Non-farm Sector (NFS)

Non-farm Sector holds the potential and promise for generating employment and increased income in the rural areas. It is a key to faster economic development of the country. Hence, NABARD takes necessary steps to develop and promote the rural area through the scheme of Rural Non-Farm Sector (RNFS). The objectives of Scheme is to be in constant touch with emerging needs for credit in rural areas for small industrial and service enterprises and respond adequately with financial packages to meet such needs both by way of refinance and direct finance and promote on an experimental basis rural entrepreneurship and enterprises in collaboration with promotional and development agencies sharing such a commitment, to introduce a bias in credit delivery and other promotional means in favour of women, weaker sections and resource poor regions and to bring about awareness on environmental impact of rural credit projects and disseminate NABARD's experiences on financing and promoting RNFS.

Under the Scheme, any unit which is in existence for at least two years will be eligible for acquisition of new machinery and equipment resulting in additional production capacity and/or improving productivity or introducing new product/product line, etc. The total cost of investment in plant and machinery including that of modernisation/renovation/expansion/diversification of the existing units to be financed should not exceed a small scale industry (SSI) unit. Manufacturing, processing and approved service sector activity (including transport vehicles, infrastructure and marketing) are eligible.

Service sector activities benefiting rural areas and having some investment in fixed assets and not purely trading in nature are eligible. Refinance up to Automatic Refinance Facility (ARF) limit only is available for service sector activities.

The refinance facilities available from NABARD can be broadly classified into investment credit and production credit.

Under the investment credit, NABARD provides refinance to eligible banks for a wide spectrum of manufacturing, processing and service sector activities. Refinance up to Rs. 15 lakh is available under Automatic Refinance Facility (ARF) and beyond that under pre-sanction procedure up to SSI limit.

The various finance schemes formulated over the years have been categorised into five distinct and compact schemes viz., i. Composite Loan Scheme ii. Integrated Loan Scheme, iii. Small Road and Water Transport Operators Scheme, iv. Pre-Sanction Procedure and v. Soft Loan Assistance for margin Money Scheme.

4.11.1 Refinancing by NABARD for NFS Scheme: The NABARD involvement in refinance for NFS scheme is dealt below. The position of disbursement throughout India and growth rate during 1982 to 2007 for NFS Scheme is furnished in Table 4.21.

Table 4.21: Disbursement under NFS Scheme

Year	Disbursements (Rs. Crore)		Share of NFS Scheme (%)	YOY Rate
	NFS Scheme	All Scheme		
1982-83	-	703	-	-
1983-84	-	892	-	-
1984-85	-	1062	-	-
1985-86	-	1192	-	-
1986-87	-	1334	-	-
1987-88	-	1482	-	-
1988-89	-	1270	-	-
1989-90	62	1702	3.64	-
1990-91	80	1904	4.20	29.03
1991-92	104	2054	5.06	30.00
1992-93	185	2359	7.84	77.88
1993-94	329	2745	11.99	77.84
1994-95	411	3011	13.65	24.92
1995-96	460	3063	15.02	11.92
1996-97	645	3523	18.31	40.22
1997-98	616	3922	15.71	-4.50
1998-99	654	4521	14.47	6.17
1999-00	837	5215	16.05	27.98

Contd...

2000-01	1022	6158	16.60	22.10
2001-02	1116	6682	16.70	9.20
2002-03	1238	7418	16.69	10.93
2003-04	2363	7605	31.07	90.87
2004-05	2542	8577	29.64	7.58
2005-06	2286	8622	26.51	-10.07
2006-07	2265	8795	25.75	-0.92

Source: NABARD Annual Reports (complied and computed)

The disbursement share of NFS scheme as regards the total to disbursement under all schemes operated by NABARD has increased over the years. From a mere 3.64 per cent in 1989-90, the figure increased to 25.75 per cent in 2006-07. During 1997-98, the disbursement to this scheme at Rs. 616 crore registered a decline of nearly 4 per cent compared to the previous year. Later the disbursement share increased to 90.87 per cent during 2003-04. This shows that non farm sector was vibrant during this period. After that, the percentage was reduced to 0.92 during 2006-07 because at present, most of the rural people want diversion from farm to non-farm activities.

4.11.2 Agency-wise Refinance by NABARD: Agency-wise disbursement by NABARD throughout India under NFS Scheme for the year ended 31st March 2007 is given in Table 4.22.

Table 4.22: Agency-wise Disbursement under NFS Scheme

Agency	Financial Assistance 2006-07	Commit-ment 2006-07	D during 2006-07	Share (%)	Cumulative D as on March 31, 2007	Share (%)
SCARDB	651	605	605	26.72	5601	30.29
CBs	1081	967	967	42.69	4499	24.33
SCBs	373	313	313	13.82	4094	22.14
RRBs	480	380	380	16.78	4294	23.22
ADFCs/ PUCBs	-	-	-	-	115	0.62
Total	2585	2265	2265	100	18488	100

D = Disbursement

Source: Statistical Statement Issued by NABARD (2006-07)

4.12 Self-help Groups (SHGs)

Self-help Groups is a concept that emerged in the direction of helping rural poor by forming groups so that they have better their living conditions through voluntary participation in thrift and credit. The main focus is on flexibility, transparency and autonomy with sensitivity and responsiveness of the participants.

Self-help Groups is a small, homogeneous affinity group of rural poor comprising agricultural labourers, small and marginal farmers, and micro entrepreneurs who have voluntarily come forward to form a group. It can be a formal or an informal group. Members of SHG save and contribute to a common fund, from which small loans are lent to the needy members as per the decision of the group. The concept underlines the principle of thrift, credit and self-help. Rural poor have the potential to save small amounts and have the inherent quality of helping themselves through mutual trust and active participation.

In 1976, Professor Mohamed Yunus of Bangladesh experimented the concept and found it a success. This led to establishment of Bangladesh Grameen Bank in 1980 which is now operating with more than 1400 branches and a corpus of more than Rs. 800 crore. The Bank does not undertake traditional banking as done by commercial banks. Similar programmes were followed by other developing countries. In India, some NGOs introduced the scheme during 1987-89. NABARD took up the scheme on pilot project basis during 1991-92 and later extended it to all states in the country. State Bank of India started providing financial assistance to SHGs from 1996-97. At present, the scheme is in operation throughout the country.

Self-help Groups activities are classified into financial, managerial and secretarial. Financial activities include encouraging thrift habit among the rural poor, lending to members and earning interest, increasing base funds, selection and financing of income generation activities, opening of deposit account with NGOs/Banks, borrowing from banks/NGOs, recovery of loans from members, and repayment of bank loans. Managerial activities include conducting regular meeting, ensuring discipline among member by imposing fines/penalties for late attendance/non attendance/late payment of thrift and loan installment, undertaking joint venture and bringing cohesion among group members, arranging training for the members, arranging backward and forward linkages for gainful activities undertaken by the members, organizing social, educational and cultural activities in the villages to bring enlightenment among rural poor and participation in SHG clusters. On the other hand secretarial activities include maintenance of records like attendance register, minutes book, loan ledger, pass book to members, ensuring transparency in group operations, developing leadership qualities among members and ensuring participatory functioning.

Characteristics of Self-help Groups are transparency in operations, resolving conflicts through collective leadership and mutual discussions, autonomous, non political and no outside influence, improving base funds by thrift, internal lending and mobilizing external funds like loans/grants/donations etc., credit decision as per consensus in group meetings and credit delivery on the spot, mutual trust and confidence, recovery through peer pressure, democratic financial management system and capacity building among members to interact with outsiders without fear or favour.

Sanction of loan to SHGs by banks is based on the quantum of savings mobilized by a SHG, but not for any specific purpose. The loans may be for consumption or production purposes. The purpose for which the group will lend to its members should be left to the common wisdom of the group. Loans to SHG for group activities should be discouraged in initial stages. However, if the initiation comes from SHG, such proposals may be carefully examined and supervised. SHGs should be encouraged to use loans for productive purposes. Internal savings of the SHG may be used for meeting emergency needs of its members. However, banks should not deny loans to eligible SHGs simply because the stated purposes are for consumption/non-productive uses.

4.12.1 Refinancing by NABARD for SHGs Scheme: The NABARD involvement in refinance for SHGs scheme is dealt below. The position of disbursement throughout India and growth rate during last 25 years for SHG scheme is furnished in Table 4.23.

Table 4.23: Disbursements under SHG Scheme

Year	Disbursements (Rs. crore)		Share of SHGs Scheme (%)	YOY Rate
	SHGs Scheme	All Scheme		
1982-83	-	703	-	-
1983-84	-	892	-	-
1984-85	-	1062	-	-
1985-86	-	1192	-	-
1986-87	-	1334	-	-
1987-88	-	1482	-	-
1988-89	-	1270	-	-
1989-90	-	1702	-	-
1990-91	-	1904	-	-
1991-92	-	2054	-	-
1992-93	-	2359	-	-
1993-94	-	2745	-	-
1994-95	-	3011	-	-
1995-96	-	3063	-	-
1996-97	-	3523	-	-
1997-98	-	3922	--	-
1998-99	-	4521	-	-
1999-00	98	5215	1.88	-
2000-01	251	6158	4.08	156.12
2001-02	395	6682	5.91	57.37
2002-03	622	7418	8.39	57.47
2003-04	705	7605	9.27	13.34
2004-05	968	8577	11.29	37.30
2005-06	1068	8622	12.39	10.33
2006-07	1293	8795	14.70	21.07

Source: NABARD Annual Reports (compiled and computed)

The amounts loaned under the SHGs scheme by NABARD were small and were often for a short period (1 to 3 months) during the period from 1990-91 to 1993-94. Later the disbursement share for SHG slowly increased to Rs. 98 crore during 1999-2000 and reached Rs 1293 crore during 2006-07. This shows that SHGs scheme is one of the vibrant refinancing schemes of NABARD. The disbursement refinancing level of NABARD depends on saving requirements and overall performance of SHGs.

4.12.2 Agency-wise Refinance by NABARD: Agency-wise disbursement by NABARD throughout India and SHG Scheme for the year ended 31st March 2007 is given in Table 4.24.

Table 4.24: Agency-wise Disbursement under SHGs Scheme

Agency	Financial Assistance 2006-07	Commit-ment 2006-07	D during 2006-07	Share (%)	Cumulative D as on March 31, 2007	Share (%)
SCARDBs	485	483	483	37.35	2238	41.10
CBs	-	-	-	-	-	-
SCBs	184	185	185	14.31	712	13.08
RRBs	626	625	625	48.34	2495	45.82
ADFCS/ PUCBS	-	-	-	-	1	0.01
Total	1295	1293	1293	100	5445	100

D = Disbursement

Source: NABARD's Statistical Statement (2001-2002)

4.13 SC/ST Action Plan and other Schemes

One of the objectives of NABARD is to enhance the socio-economic conditions of weaker sections of the society through supporting schemes. NABARD provides refinance support for loans extended by financial institutions under the SC/ST action plans. Keeping in view the relative backgrounds of SC/ST communities, special care has been devoted to them in the formulation and implementation of development programmes. Essentially, the action plans of NABARD are production-oriented and area specific in nature, and, therefore they benefit all categories of farmers in the same communities. The action plan has been, carefully reviewed to ascertain that maximum benefits accrue to SC/ST population. NABARD has been providing 100 per cent automatic refinance to all financial agencies in respect of composite loans to SC/ST farmers. The details of NABARD refinance assistance throughout India and growth in the same rate during the last eight years is given in Table 4.25.

Table 4.25: Disbursements to SC/ST Action Plan

Year	Disbursements (Rs. Crore)		Share of SC/ST Action Plan (%)	YOY rate
	SC/ST Action Plan	All Scheme		
1982-83	-	703	-	-
1983-84	-	892	-	-
1984-85	-	1062	-	-
1985-86	-	1192	-	-
1986-87	-	1334	-	-
1987-88	-	1482	-	-
1988-89	-	1270	-	-
1989-90	-	1702	-	-
1990-91	-	1904	-	-
1991-92	-	2054	-	-
1992-93	-	2359	-	-
1993-94	-	2745	-	-
1994-95	-	3011	-	-
1995-96	71	3063	2.32	-
1996-97	96	3523	2.72	35.21
1997-98	112	3922	2.86	16.67
1998-99	106	4521	2.34	-5.36
1999-00	109	5215	2.09	2.83
2000-01	100	6158	1.62	-8.26
2001-02	130	6682	1.95	30.00
2002-03	112	7418	1.51	-13.85
2003-04	73	7605	0.96	-34.82
2004-05	80	8577	0.93	9.59
2005-06	70	8622	0.81	-12.50
2006-07	28	8795	0.32	-60.00

Source: NABARD Annual Reports (compiled and computed)

The separate figures of refinance disbursement for period

from 1990-1991 to 1995-95 are not available. The refinance disbursements during 11 years since 1995-96 recorded growth up to during 2001-02 after which it reduced to Rs. 28 crore.

4.13.1 Agency-wise Refinance by NABARD: Agency-wise disbursement by NABARD throughout India for SC/ST scheme for the year ended 31st March 2007 is given in Table 4.26.

Table 4.26: Agency–wise Disbursement under SC/ST Scheme

Agency	Financial Assistance 2006-07	Commit-ment 2006-07	D during 2006-07	Share (%)	Cumulative D as on March 31, 2007	Share (%)
SCARDBs	-	-	-	-	16	1.57
CBs	17	18	18	64.28	417	41.00
SCBs	1	1	1	3.57	71	6.98
RRBs	9	9	9	32.14	513	50.44
ADFCS/ PUCBS	-	-	-	-	-	-
	27	28	28	100	1017	100

D = Disbursement

Source: Statistical Statement Issued by NABARD (2006-07)

4.14 Other Schemes

NABARD refinance under the head "**others**" includes loan for rural godowns, two wheelers, homestead farming, contract farming, bullock-carts, sericulture, seed project, animal husbandry (others), agri-clinics and agribusiness, rural housing and other seasonal requirements of farmers like loan for purchasing of fertilizers and other minor agricultural activities. The quantum, interest and repayment period of loan are decided by NABARD from time to time.

4.14.1 Agri-clinic and Agri-business: The main objectives of the scheme is to augment support and extension services for agriculture, to provide a package of soil and input testing facilities and other consultancy services, to strengthen transfer of technology and extension services and provide self employment opportunities to technically trained persons. NABARD provides refinance for horticulture, animal husbandry, forestry, dairy, veterinary, and poultry under this scheme.

4.14.2 Bio-technology in Agriculture: NABARD provides refinance for any technique that uses living organisms to help improve plants and animals by developing micro-organisms such as yeast in brewing, baking etc.

4.14.3 Green House Technology: The concept of commercial Green House cultivation is rather new to India. This is basically used for floriculture production and also for taking up production of certain high value crops. In many cases, Green House technology is a part of other technologies like micro propagation. NABARD also provides refinance for Green House technology.

4.14.4 Vermiculture: Vermiculture is an aspect of biotechnology, which involves rearing of earthworms. Earthworms are long regarded as friends of farmers, as their presence in the soil improves the quality and productivity of crops. NABARD provides refinance for vermiculture too.

4.14.5 Land Purchase Scheme: NABARD has the provision of refinance to small and marginal farmers for purchase of land, who are existing borrowers.

4.14.6 Refinance for Two Wheelers: NABARD provides financial assistance to farmers for purchase of two wheelers to deliver the produced agricultural goods to markets easily. Moreover, the financial assistance is also available for purchase of bullock-carts.

4.14.7 Sericulture: In order to meet the challenges of globalization and economic liberalization, steps have been taken to enhance the competitiveness of Indian sericulture. These include cultivation of higher quality of mulberry, high-tech sericulture, precision silk, manufacturing and export oriented ventures.

NABARD is providing financial assistance for major projects related to sericulture which includes cultivation of silkworm food plants silk worm rearing, silk reeling and other post cocoon processes such as twisting, dyeing, weaving, printing and finishing.

The technical feasibility of the sericulture project, financial viability and generation of incremental income to ultimate borrowers, thereby enabling them to have a reasonable surplus after repayment of the loan instalments are the necessary conditions to be satisfied for sanctioning of the investment credit.

The period of loan ranges between 3 and 15 years depending on the purpose of loan. The refinance is usually 90 per cent to 95 percent of the sericulture project cost. The financial institutions and beneficiaries themselves will meet the balance. The quantum of refinance to be released by NABARD to SCARDB, SCB, RRB and CB are 95 per cent, 90 per cent, 90 per cent and 90 per cent respectively.

The NABARD refinance disbursement position throughout India and growth rate during last twelve years for "other schemes" is furnished in Table 4.27.

Table 4.27: Disbursement under Other Schemes

Year	Disbursements (Rs. crore)		Share of Others (%)	YOY rate
	Others Scheme	All Scheme		
1982-83	16	703	2.28	
1983-84	24	892	2.69	50
1984-85	32	1062	3.01	33.33
1985-86	40	1192	3.36	25
1986-87	40	1334	3.00	0
1987-88	41	1482	2.77	2.5
1988-89	30	1270	2.36	-26.83
1989-90	56	1702	3.29	86.67
1990-91	54	1904	2.84	-3.57
1991-92	67	2054	3.26	24.07
1992-93	93	2359	3.94	38.81
1993-94	53	2745	1.93	-43.01

Contd...

1994-95	53	3011	1.76	0
1995-96	179	3063	5.84	237.74
1996-97	123	3523	3.49	-31.28
1997-98	103	3922	2.63	-16.26
1998-99	151	4521	3.34	46.60
1999-00	232	5215	4.45	53.64
2000-01	159	6158	2.58	-31.47
2001-02	741	6682	11.09	366.04
2002-03	1465	7418	19.75	97.71
2003-04	1309	7605	17.21	-10.65
2004-05	1059	8577	12.35	-19.10
2005-06	708	8622	8.21	-33.14
2006-07	632.5	8795	7.19	-10.66

Source: NABARD Annual Report (compiled and computed)

The amounts loaned under "other schemes" by NABARD were started in 1982-83 at an amount of Rs. 16 crore and reached the amount at Rs 632.5 crore during 2006-07.

During the periods of twenty five years, the refinance assistance under the scheme declined only during 1988-89, 1990-91, 1993-94, 1996-97, 1997-98, 2000-01 and 2003-04 to 2006-07.

The share of "other schemes" in all schemes operated by NABARD started increasing slowly from 2.28 per cent during 1982-83 to 19.75 per cent during 2002-2003 after that it reached 7.19 during 2006-07.

4.14.8 Agency-wise Refinance by NABARD: Agency-wise disbursement by NABARD throughout India for other schemes for the year ended 31st March 2007 in given in Table 4.28.

4.15 Analysis of Refinance by NABARD

NABARD's refinance assistance to various financial institutions, at all-India level, is analyzed below. This analysis is made with regard to various aspects like year-wise, region-wise, state-wise, purpose-wise, financial institution-wise, and number of schemes-wise.

Table 4.28: Agency Wise Disbursement under Other Scheme (Rs. crore)

Agency	Financial Assistance 2001-02	Commit-ment 2001-02	D during 2001-02	Share (%)	Cumulative D as on March 31, 2002	Share (%)
SCARDBs	38	38	38	6.71	837	14.81
CBs	353	331	330	58.30	3105	54.94
SCBs	161	150	150	26.50	892	15.78
RRBs	52	47	48	8.48	815	14.42
ADFCS/ PUCBS	-	-	-	-	3	0.05
	604	566	566	100	5652	100

D = Disbursement

Source: Statistical Statement Issued by NABARD

4.15.1 Year-wise Refinance Disbursement of NABARD: Table 4.29 shows, the year-wise refinance disbursement of NABARD to all financial institutions at all-India level. NABARD started its refinance assistances from its inception in 1982-83.

4.15.2 Region-wise Refinance Disbursement of NABARD: The region-wise refinance disbursement of NABARD is presented in Table 4.30 Among the region-wise distribution, so far the maximum amount of refinance was disbursed to Southern region (29 per cent) followed by Northern region (22 per cent), Central region (21 per cent), Western region (14 per cent), Eastern region (12 per cent) and North Eastern region (2 per cent).

4.15.3 State-wise Refinance Disbursement: State-wise refinance disbursement by NABARD is presented in Table 4.31.

4.15.4 Purpose-wise Refinance Disbursement: Purpose-wise refinance disbursement by NABARD is presented in Table 4.32.

4.15.5 Financial Institutions-wise Refinance: NABARD's financial assistance through different financial institutions is presented in Table 4.33.

4.15.6 Purpose-wise Number of Schemes Sanctioned: Table 4.34 presents the purpose-wise number of schemes sanctioned during 1999-2000 to 2006-07.

Table 4.29: Year-wise Refinance Disbursement of NABARD (Rs. crore)

Year	Disbursement at all India level	Increased/Decrease Percentage
1982-83	703	-
1983-84	892	27
1984-85	1,062	19
1985-86	1,192	12
1986-87	1,334	12
1987-88	1,482	11
1988-89	1,270	-14
1989-90	1,702	34
1990-91	1,904	12
1991-92	2,054	8
1992-93	2,359	15
1993-94	2,745	16
1994-95	3,011	10
1995-96	3,063	2
1996-97	3,523	15
1997-98	3,922	11
1998-99	4,521	15
1999-00	5,215	15
2000-01	6,158	18
2001-02	6,682	8
2002-03	7,418	11
2003-04	7,605	2
2004-05	8,577	13
2005-06	8,622	0.5
2006-07	8,795	2

Table 4.30: Region-wise Refinance Disbursement of NABARD (Rs. crore)

Year	N	NE	E	C	W	S	Total
1982 – 83	190	8	90	151	80	184	703
1983 – 84	242	9	96	190	128	227	892
1984 – 85	241	14	126	238	153	289	1061
1985 – 86	250	22	148	256	175	341	1192
1986 – 87	286	26	187	271	183	381	1334
1987 – 88	285	34	217	308	216	422	1482
1988 – 89	191	25	167	292	181	414	1270
1989 – 90	283	42	198	392	270	517	1702
1990 – 91	290	49	204	475	328	558	1904
1991 – 92	307	40	228	540	349	590	2054
1992 – 93	368	36	249	565	402	738	2358
1993 – 94	453	40	255	585	499	912	2744
1994 – 95	520	51	274	628	554	984	3011
1995 – 96	566	68	285	632	536	977	3064
1996 – 97	718	108	383	635	564	1115	3523
1997 – 98	889	117	432	701	571	1212	3922
1998 – 99	1121	142	491	874	642	1251	4521
1999 – 00	1231	110	575	1015	834	1450	5215
2000 - 01	1377	131	714	1276	945	1714	6157
2001 - 02	1419	80	793	1454	1075	1862	6683
2002 - 03	1619	120	814	1684	971	2210	7418
2003 - 04	1781	123	1069	1673	795	2164	7605
2004 - 05	2248	219	1035	2095	788	2192	8577
2005 - 06	2152	147	1057	2307	893	2065	8621
2006 – 07	2111	168	1103	1696	1007	2711	8796

N = **Northern; NE = North Eastern; E = Eastern; C = Central; W = Western; S = Southern**

Table 4.31: State-wise Refinance Disbursement

(Rs. crore)

	2001-02	2002-03	2003-04	2004-05	2005-06	2006-07
Chandigarh	0.1	6	7	4	0.14	0.02
Delhi	6	7	82	8	8	8
Hariyana	407	478	508	593	598	582
HP	127	176	212	157	167	146
J&K	39	49	7	27	22	26
Punjab	437	573	676	1041	949	880
Rajasthan	405	330	362	415	408	469
Arunachal Paradesh	3	7	7	10	3	1.6
Assam	48	69	73	133	75	93
Manipur	0.5	5	2	9	8	8
Meghalaya	8	9	9	12	12	14
Mizoram	9	16	17	36	22	24
Nagaland	2	2	1	2	1	2
Tripura	9	10	12	16	27	20
Andaman & Nicobar	3	4	5	5	0.3	7
Bihar	97	82	97	176	117	168
Jharkhand	45	39	45	48	52	62
Orissa	320	269	308	322	280	344
Sikkim	3	4	-	9	9	5
West Bengal	324	415	613	474	598	522
MP	344	410	370	524	527	442
Uttar Pradesh	1027	1175	1221	1473	1548	1122
Chhattisgarh	60	64	60	80	200	85
Uttaranchal	22	35	20	17	30	45
Goa	19	19	13	7	14	13
Gujarat	314	362	324	304	279	593
Maharashtra	741	589	458	476	599	401
Andhra Pradesh	602	761	607	895	752	966
Karnataka	343	453	473	455	453	699
Kerala	373	308	342	448	415	517
Pondicherry	4	5	9	5	16	5
Tamil Nadu	539	683	733	389	429	522
Lakshadweep	0.9	-	-	-	0.12	0.75

Table 4.32: Purpose-wise Refinance Disbursement

(Rs. crore)

	2001-02	2002-03	2003-04	2004-05	2005-06	2006-07
Minor Irrigation	691	854	651	680	541	671
Land Development	135	251	185	291	637	651
Farm Mechanigation	1359	993	827	1055	1713	1857
Plantation & Horticulture	280	292	251	236	322	314
Poultry/Sheep/ Goat/Piggry	176	186	280	361	231	140
Fisheries	36	35	23	26	38	38
Diary Development	821	909	669	754	695	504
Storage & Market Yarob	227	48	25	33	52	36
Forestry	16	12	11	9	7	8
Bio-Gas Plant	-	-	-	-	-	0.8
Non-Form Sector	1116	1238	2363	2542	2286	2265
SC/ST Action Plan	130	112	73	80	70	28
Others	241	696	1309	1059	708	566
IRDB/SGSY	559	401	229	483	252	355
Self help groups	395	622	705	968	1068	1293
Animal husbandry others	-	-	-	-	-	66
Agriclinics & Agribusiness	-	-	-	-	-	0.5
Rural Housing	500	769	-	-	-	-

Table 4.33: Financial Institutions-wise Refinance

(Rs. crore)

Name of the institutions	2001-02	2002-03	2003-04	2004-05	2005-06	2006-07
SCARDBs	2732	2853	2544	2709	2082	1743
CBs	1608	1241	1714	2569	4028	4569
SCBs	1089	1784	1736	1244	1174	1131
RRBs	1178	1539	1589	2049	1332	1353
ADFCs/ PUCBs	76	1.3	22	5	6	-

Table 4.34: Purpose-wise Number of Schemes Sanctioned during 2001-02 to 2006-07

	2001-02	2002-03	2003-04	2004-05	2005-06	2006-07
Minor Irrigation	664	198	7144	60	10719	41
Land Development	10	9	15	6	5356	8
Farm Mechanization	-	-	-	-	7674	-
Plantation/ Horticulture	51	20	17	9	185	3
Poultry/Sheep/ Piggery	8	5	3	1	1602	2
Fisheries	7	-	-	1	78	2
Diary Development	22	25	6	7	7847	-
Storage Market Yard	183	55	47	8	37	9
Forestry	5	7	116	48	1	1
Global Gas plant	5	1	-	-	8	-
Non-Farm Sector	3	3	275	10	17705	2
Seed Project	-	-	-	-	-	-
SC/ST Action Plan	-	-	-	-	2000	-
Others	3	174	2	10	251	1
SGSY	-	-	-	-	6405	-
Animal Husbandry, others	-	-	1	-	381	-
SHG	-	-	-	-	7750	-
Agriclinics & Agribusiness	-	-	-	1	-	-
Total	961	497	7626	161	67999	69

5

Agriculture Insurance in India: Recent Initiatives

Agriculture insurance is much wider in scope and content and includes insurance of seed, cattle, horticulture, plantations, forestry, sericulture, aquaculture, poultry, viniculture and all such activities which are allied to agriculture. In its wider connotation, it should cover all operations commencing from sowing of seeds to marketing of final products which are connected to agriculture. It will also include all the capital equipments used during different stages of agricultural operations such as tractors, threshing machines, drought animals, pumpsets, processing plants etc. From this angle, agriculture insurance can be treated as synonymous with rural insurance.

5.1 Agriculture Insurance: Policy Issues

5.1.1 Role of the State: While agricultural insurance has an important role in supporting the development of modern agriculture, its introduction and proliferation must not be left to the courage of individual insurers. If governments wish to see agricultural insurance as a standard component of modern agriculture, then they have to provide financial means substantial enough to make available excess reinsurance covers to the direct insurers. They may do this through capitalising a reinsurer, acting as a substantive participant in a reinsurance role or providing subsidies to make up for the gap between direct rates and international reinsurance rates.

Governments, at the Central and State levels, have a distinct role to play in facilitating the development of agricultural insurance. Their concerns can be broadly summarised as follows:

- An economic and trading environment congenial to the agricultural sector has to be created. This would include supply of various inputs, transportation and marketing arrangements, creation or improvement of infrastructural facilities necessary for successful operations, and remunerative prices for the produce wherever the government has a say in their determination. This is not the case in a number of developing countries and consequently, agricultural activities continue to remain in a depressed condition. It is true that this is a major policy and macro-economic issue which extends beyond the scope of agricultural insurance, at the same time, it needs to be emphasised that agricultural insurance can prosper only to the extent the activity or the property it seeks to insure is economically viable.
- A legal and fiscal framework conducive to the functioning of the insurance system has to be provided. This would include suitable provision for incorporation of mutuals and co-operatives under the insurance statute, and liberalisation in the insurance sector so that the number of players can be increased. While the private sector companies have many handicaps in the area of agricultural insurance, they can do better if supported by the government. Better enforcement of rules and regulations relating to agricultural production is also necessary for agricultural insurance to be effective. Agricultural risks are particularly exposed to natural catastrophes. Since such events occur only once in a while, a part of the savings of a year has to be funded in a reserve to meet liability in the year when a catastrophe strikes. The tax laws, however, usually do not permit such funding to be tax deductible, and the savings of a year are treated as profit and taxed in the normal manner.
- Support of financial institutions to agricultural insurance is vital. Further the concerned authorities should make available the foreign exchange required for reinsurance.

- The insurance sector may have to be strengthened by requiring enhancement of the capital base of insurance organisation so that larger risks can be assumed. The government can also provide much needed support to the insurance sector in developing skilled manpower by supporting specialised education and training, and in enhancing awareness of insurance.
- Infrastructural facilities for accurate and timely collection of meteorological data as related to agriculture, activities for control of diseases related to livestock, poultry fish etc. and support services such as extension services may need to be strengthened.
- The developmental aspect of insurance supervision and regulation may require taking initiatives to overcome inertia by generation of the necessary impulses and provision of motivation. It can be argued that when credit institutions can be influenced, or required, to lend for agricultural operations as priority sector, the insurance industry can also be made to pay greater attention to agricultural and rural risks.

Agricultural insurance has a clear and definite role to play in the development of the rural economy, which will in turn strengthen the national economy. At the same time, the limitations of agricultural insurance should be recognised, and it should not be idealised or romanticised. Insurance is only one of several financial services, and even in the industrial and commercial sectors its role is supportive. Insurance should not be seen or promoted as a solitary effort but as a component of services that need to be extended to the agricultural sector. In fact, agricultural insurance can be most effective if it is conceived and implemented as a part of this broader framework.

Agricultural insurance is an important instrument in the strategy of risk management. When properly implemented, it results in a process of identification of risks, their control, avoidance or reduction. This is obviously in the interests of insurance companies and they are generally eager to promote it. Apart from the financial interests of insurance companies, risk management has a broader social aspect as it leads to reduction in wastage of economic resources and prevents environmental degradation.

National insurance markets in most developing countries have been established only in the last two decades and it is not surprising that, by and large, private sector insurance companies have not so far become involved in agricultural insurance to any significant extent. The time has now come for private sector insurance companies to extend the boundaries of their operations and pay attention to the insurance needs of the agricultural and rural sectors. They are, however, unlikely to be effective in providing insurance to the traditional or subsistence sector for three basic reasons.

- Their main line of business, servicing the industrial and commercial sector, absorbs their financial and personnel resources. The needs of this sector are also growing. Substantial ground has yet to be covered, particularly if the markets are opened to foreign insurers.
- Private sector insurance companies in developing countries are often constrained by a small capital base, and are unlikely to attract additional resources for underwriting agricultural insurance.
- Prospects of assured profits in this line of activity are not promising.

However, to the extent that private insurance companies are willing to be involved in the exercise, they should be encouraged. This has to be done at several levels and should, inter alia, consist of providing a suitable legal framework, offering a level playing field vis-à-vis public sector institutions and setting up incentive mechanisms.

5.1.2 Scope of Private Sector Companies: Substantial opportunities exist for extending insurance to the commercial and specialised production systems. These sectors are growing and include medium-size farms, those supplying their output to processing units, plantations of tea, coffee, cocoa, rubber and oilseeds, social forestry, cultivation of seeds, horticulture, poultry farming, aquaculture, greenhouses, hydrophonic vegetable production and non-traditional or specialised items for export such as production of vegetables, fruit and flowers under strict quality control. It is also within the reach of private sector companies to provide livestock insurance to groups of cattle kept commercially by dairies, as also to individual farmers. These risks are small and manageable. Private companies have a distinct and special, as also a positive, role to play in these areas. They would have sufficient flexibility in devising suitable products, and in formulating servicing arrangements. It is felt that systematic and organised efforts to extend insurance to commercialised agricultural sectors have not yet been made. The biggest hurdle is apprehension of the unknown.

However, new and potentially risky lines of business such as offshore oil rigs and satellite insurance have been successfully managed and similar inventiveness and detailed planning may be applied to meeting the insurance needs of the rural and agricultural sectors. Besides expansion of business, some of them would be able to create a niche for themselves by specialising in a particular line. This may help in expanding and opening up domestic markets.

5.1.3 Role of Parastatal Insurance Organisations: The possibilities and the desirability of private sector companies taking up agricultural and rural insurance particularly for commercialised sectors does not imply underestimating the role of the parastatal bodies already engaged in this line. They have laid the foundations and have built some infrastructure and expertise, and this should not be lost. Private sector companies have the inherent handicap of a limited capital base. Parastatal bodies, however, must persevere to make their schemes more effective. However, as far as agricultural insurance is concerned it is clear that financial discipline and accountability have to be injected into the operations of parastatal bodies. There is a clear need for the commercialisation of their operations.

Taking a broader view of agricultural insurance in its entirely, three factors that have inhibited its development are the following.

- Lack of technical knowledge of the operational processes involved.
- Inadequate infrastructure and agricultural support services.
- Difficulties in product development.

Agricultural insurance can succeed if companies adopt a technical approach, and the services of veterinarians and other specialists are used. The skills of the persons engaged would also require upgrading from time to time by organising training programmes and exposing them to international experiences. A viable delivery and servicing system to give shape to the effort has to be created in the form of a network of branches, a trained and motivated marketing cadre dedicated to the development of the rural sector, and support services such as qualified and experienced personnel for survey and assessment of losses.

Many developing countries also need help in product development and improvement. While some studies have been made and literature has been published on crop insurance, there is hardly any literature on livestock, poultry, aquaculture, and other lines of agricultural insurance. There is an urgent need for an enhanced level of exchange of information and experiences. The establishment of a data bank to collect the details of various models developed to catalogue possible options and alternatives and to collect and update basic statistics in the field of agricultural insurance should be considered. Research on various aspects of agricultural insurance is also needed.

5.1.4 Market-sponsored Companies: One of the limited factors in the growth of agricultural insurance in developing countries has been the inadequacy of the capital base and underwriting capacity of insurance enterprises especially in the private sector. To mitigate the situation, several possibilities can be explored. Mutuals and co-operatives may be encouraged in rural areas, and the scope of those already existing can be expanded to provide insurance services to farmers and others. This would reduce pressure on more formally constituted organisation. Schemes geared towards local needs may have better results and would be more likely to reduce problems related to asymmetric information. Further, pools can be established to share the underwriting capacity and marketing talents of existing insurance companies. And, lastly, depending on local conditions, the establishment of a market-sponsored agricultural insurance company could be considered. It will have the benefit of the resources, marketing organisation and insurance expertise of the insurance companies in the market. Participation of other financial institutions and related organisations should be sought. Involvement of a foreign organisation specialising in agricultural insurance could also be considered. The possibility of obtaining the symbolic support of the State by way of a minority shareholding could be examined.

5.1.5 Reinsurance: An external possibility of enhancing underwriting capacity is the utilisation of the reinsurance market. Reinsurance also provides a degree of financial discipline. However, reinsurance support is available only for technically viable programmes. Furthermore, the international reinsurance capacity for agricultural risks in developing countries is limited, particularly for natural catastrophes. This, in fact, is one of the major factors inhibiting the development of agricultural insurances. Serious thought needs to be given to this aspect. The State can play a significant role by creating additional reinsurance facilities, either by encouraging the establishment of reinsurance companies or directly providing reinsurance.

In conclusion it may be stated that agricultural insurance is very sensitive in nature. Although, basic principles are commonly applicable, agricultural schemes should be in conformity with the particular environment of the country. Its growth and development requires constant and careful nurturing. Mutual interaction and sharing of experience of development countries can be helpful for its healthy growth.

As a concluding comment, it may be stated that the difficulties to be overcome in introducing and propagating agricultural insurance in developing countries should not be underestimated. They are many and formidable. In a number of countries only a few lines have been introduced, and in others while schemes have been devised their scope is limited. A more purposeful thrust will require conscious and concerted efforts and the process should be initiated soon.

5.2 Advent and Development of Agriculture/Rural Insurance in India

The general insurance business was nationalised in India in the year 1973. The private companies numbering around 106 were grouped in the following companies: National Insurance Co. Ltd., New India Assurance Co. Ltd., Oriental Insurance Co. Ltd., and United India Insurance Co. Ltd. General Insurance Corporation of India (GIC) was formed as Holding Company for the above 4 insurance companies formed after nationalisation. The 4 general insurance companies are the subsidiaries of GIC of India.

Before nationalisation the general insurance business was transacted mainly in the metro cities and urban centres. The business transacted in rural areas was almost nil. There were no exclusive insurance policies to cater to the requirements of rural India. The purpose of nationalisation of general insurance business was to spread the general insurance throughout India including all rural areas. With this in mind, GIC opened the branches of their subsidiary companies in all the districts in India. By this process, there was not a single district that can be treated as *no branch district*.

As a first step, GIC designed the following policies in the year 1974-75 to cater to the needs of rural people: cattle insurance, Janata Personal Accident Insurance and Agricultural Pump Set Insurance.

The public sector banks were advised to loan money to the priority sector that would cover advances for cattle and agricultural pump sets on a large scale. The Janata Personal Accident Policy was envisaged with a very low premium so that it would be affordable to the rural man to take the Personal Accident Policy with a low premium. In a number of cases, the banks who were advancing money for the rural activities took Master Policies to cover all their loanees.

Another land mark in general insurance was the advent of crop insurance. The crop insurance was commenced in the year 1985 by GIC as an implementing agency on behalf of Central and State Governments. Unlike the traditional and rural non-traditional business, wherein the premium is credited to the insurance companies and the claims are settled by them, in crop insurance the premium is credited to the Central and State Governments in agreed proportion and the claims are borne by Central and State Governments in the same proportion.

Arising out of crop insurance, the demand was made on the general insurance industry to design the insurance cover for the areas like plantation, and floriculture. The rubber plantations, tea and coffee, eucalyptus, poplar trees and tobacco were brought under insurance cover. This was extended later to floriculture wherein the roses and orchids were brought under insurance coverage.

The designing of some rural insurance covers was quite challenging to the industry. There was no precedence in designing the cover for poultry, inland and brackish water fish and prawn, silkworm, and honeybees. The cover designed in the industry for these sectors was comprehensive and there was no parallel in other countries. Therefore, Indian general insurance industry is acknowledged as highly innovative in designing rural insurance covers.

Apart from the formulation of new covers, the marketing

of such covers was more challenging to the industry. India is a large agricultural country with rural economy as its main stake, a very strong infrastructure is required to market these products all over India. To some extent the branches, particularly those in semi-urban and rural areas served the purpose. The marketing force of the industry consisted of development officers and agents. For obvious reasons, the industry could not reach the rural areas through these marketing forces. Therefore, industry required alternative strategies.

Hence, banks were directed to make advances to priority sector in a substantial manner. The advances by the banks in priority sector cover agriculture and also many subsidiary operations like animal husbandry, fisheries, sericulture etc. The banks are used by the general insurance companies as the nodal point to extend rural insurance coverage. The Master Policies are issued in favour of banks for their cattle advances. The certificates are issued by insurance companies under the Master Policy and given to the banks and loanees as proof of insurance.

The other resourceful nodal points are co-operative societies like dairy and milk co-operative societies, District Rural Development Agencies (DRDAs). DRDAs are monitoring the subsidy programmes of the Government. Many subsidy programmes are formulated by the Central Government for small/marginal farmers, drought prone areas, scheduled caste and tribes and backward classes and such other category of farmers below the poverty line. The general insurance industry came forward to support Central and State Governments in their various social welfare programmes by designing specific and tailor-made insurance coverages apart from the standard insurance policies.

In spite of the attempts made by the Government-owned GIC, the Indian insurance industry is yet to penetrate the rural market in a big way. The opening up of the insurance sector to private players is expected to generate increased activities in rural India by the companies. The new private insurance companies will do well to perform their role in promoting rural insurance as per the stipulations of Insurance Regulatory and Development Authority (IRDA). The scope for rural business is unlimited. Besides marketing the existing products the companies can explore the avenues to innovate new rural insurance covers.

5.3 Comprehensive Crop Insurance Scheme (CCIS)

Agriculture is influenced by vagaries of weather. Large-scale crop failures have very adverse effect on the economic conditions of the farmers. Such crop failures occur every year in one part of the country or the other due to natural calamities such as drought, flood, cyclone etc. As a result of such crop failure, farmers in general and small farmers in particular not only lose their current crop but are also left with no money to invest in the next crop season. If they have taken loans, their credit worthiness is also adversely affected. The impact of crop failure is devastating where size of land holding is small and their numbers are large.

There is, therefore, great need of crop insurance as one of the major risk transfer measures and crop insurance can certainly to some extent absorb disastrous effects of large-scale crop failures.

Realising the need of crop insurance, some countries have designed and introduced crop insurance schemes but much more needs to be done. Private insurers are not much interested because of the nature of catastrophic risks involved. Whatever schemes are in operation are mainly with Government support. It is a challenge for all concerned to design a viable scheme. Co-operation and interaction in this regard can perhaps help in finding some solution. The situation is not much different in respect of some of other classes of agricultural/rural insurance.

An important issue relates to the number of crops which should be covered under the ambit of crop insurance. In a country, where the agriculture is confined to one or two crops, the choice is quite limited. The insurance coverage will be extended to only these crops. But the choice becomes difficult in a country where multiple crops are grown. Since in most of the countries crop insurance operates under government subsidy, government would encourage insurance of those crops which are important to the economy in the sense that they may either be the main cereals, or source of raw material to agro-based processing industries whose products are exported constituting main source of foreign exchange earning.

In case crop insurance is carried out by private insurance companies without government support and subsidy, they may opt for those crops in which methods of production are stable and standardised. With methods of production being modern and stable, the variations in output will be minimum except those caused by external factors such as cyclone, floods, hailstorm etc. For these crops it is easy for insurance companies to calculate the risks which may be caused by internal factors and help them in calculating actuarial rates for insurance covers.

In India, the first systematic crop insurance scheme implemented on a wider scheme known as Comprehensive Crop Insurance Scheme (CCIS) was introduced in 1985. CCIS was conceived as an instrument of risk management in agriculture, as a tool to provide relief to the farmers sustaining losses to the crops during natural catastrophe and calamities, and as an integral part of policy package for overall growth of agriculture and its productivity. It was also used as a tool to support and stimulate production of desired commodities such as food grains, pulses and oil seeds. The scheme covered the crops of rice, wheat, millets (including maize) oilseeds and pulses and covered all the farmers availing loan from financial institutions for raising the above crops. The scheme was voluntary in nature and it was left to the wisdom of state governments to opt for the scheme and the districts in which they wanted the scheme to operate. Insurance coverage was built in as a part of crop loan.

Salient features of the scheme were the following.

- **Crops Covered**: paddy, wheat and millets, oilseeds and pulses.
- **Premium Rates (Insurance Coverage):** 2 per cent of sum insured for cereals, millets and 1 per cent for oilseeds and pulses. Subsidy to small and marginal farmers: 50 per cent for premium.
- **Farmers Covered:** All farmers availing of crop loans from co-operative credit institutions, commercial banks and regional rural banks for raising the aforesaid crops in the notified areas.
- **Area Approach:** The scheme operated in defined areas for each crop as may be notified by the Crop Insurance Fund Committee constituted by each State Government. A defined Area meant a district/tehsil/taluka, block or other smaller contiguous area.
- **Nature of Coverage:** All risks coverage. If the actual average yield per hectare of the insured crop for the defined area determined on the basis of crop cutting experiments in the insured season, fell short of the specified threshold yield, all the insured farmers growing that crop in the defined area were deemed to have suffered shortfall in their respective yields and the scheme provided coverage against such contingency.
- **Limit of Coverage (Sum Insured):** The sum insured per insured farmer was 150 per cent of the loan disbursed for growing the crop in the defined area during the insured season, which was subsequently reduced to 100 per cent of crop loan subject to maximum of Rs. 10,000 per farmer per season.
- Participation of the States in the scheme was voluntary. Risk sharing between Central and State Governments was in the ratio of 2:1.

5.3.1 Drawbacks of CCIS: The following were the main shortcomings of the scheme.

- It covered only loanee farmers, leaving non-loanee farmers, who constitute majority, out of the purview of the Scheme.
- As the Scheme covered only food crops and oilseeds, farmers growing commercial crops like sugarcane, potato, chillies, cotton etc. are left out of purview of the scheme.
- Sum-insured limit of Rs.10,000 was too low to cover the input cost incurred by a farmer.
- High claim ratio because of low, flat premium rates.

Demands were made from time to time by the farming community as well as the implementing States for improving the scope and contents of CCIS. These demands included the following.

- Bringing more crops into the purview of crop insurance.
- Extending its scope to cover all farmers (both loanee and non-loanee).
- Increasing the sum insured.
- Lowering the unit area of insurance.

5.3.2 Experimental Crop Insurance Scheme (ECIS): During the course of implementation of CCIS, a new scheme, viz. Experimental Crop Insurance Scheme (ECIS) was introduced during rabi 1997-98 season for one year, subject to review after the first cropping season. ECIS covered all the marginal and small farmers, both loanee and non-loanee, growing wheat, paddy millets (including maize) oilseeds and pulses in 24 selected districts of 8 States. The entire amount of premium was borne by Central and State Governments. Share of Central and State Governments for premium and claims was in the ratio of 4:1. Other features of the scheme were common with that of CCIS.

5.4 National Agriculture Insurance Scheme (NAIS)

In order to make up for the deficiencies of CCIS, a new scheme called, National Agricultural Insurance Scheme (NAIS) was introduced from rabi 1999-2000, replacing CCIS. General Insurance Corporation of India was the implementing agency for CCIS. Under NAIS there is provision for setting up an exclusive organisation for implementation of the scheme and until the new set up is created, GIC will continue to function as the implementing agency. Agricultural Insurance Company of India Ltd. (AICIL) which was incorporated in December 2002 and started operating from April, 2003 took over the implementation of NAIS.

The scheme covers all the farmers, loanee and non-loanee, including share-croppers and tenant farmers. The scheme is compulsory for loanee farmers and voluntary for non-loanee farmers. The scheme covers all food crops and oilseeds as well as annual horticultural/commercial crops. It is a multi-peril scheme covering all natural and non- preventive risks. The sum insured could extend to the value of threshold yield of the insured crop at the option of insured farmers. However, a farmer may also insure his crop beyond the value of threshold yield up to 150 per cent of average yield notified on payment of premium at commercial rates. In case of loanee farmers, the sum insured would at least be equal to the amount of crop loan advanced.

In short, the salient features of the scheme are the following.

- Coverage of all farmers (both loanee and non-loanee) including share croppers and tenant farmers.
- Coverage of annual commercial/horticultural crops besides food crops and oilseeds.
- Basically an all-risk insurance, covering all natural and non-preventable risks.
- As against limit of sum insured of Rs. 10,000 farmer per season, sum insured can be as high as 150 per cent of average yield.
- Experimenting assessment of crop losses on individual basis for localised calamities like hailstorm, landslide, flood etc.
- As against the flat rates charged under CCIS, premium rates are actuarial for annual commercial/horticultural

crops.

- Small and marginal farmers are entitled for 50 per cent subsidy in premium which is to be phased out over a period of 5 years.
- Claims over certain limits are to be borne by the Government and shared equally by Central and implementing State Governments. For this purpose, corpus fund with equal contribution by Central and State will be formed.

5.4.1 Operational Modalities: NAIS is a multi-agency scheme and Central Government, State Governments, financial institutions and GIC play their roles in implementation. State Governments constitute State Level Coordination Committees on Crop Insurance (SLCCCI) headed by Agricultural Production Commissioner and includes senior officers of the State Government, viz. Secretary (Agriculture), Secretary (Finance), Director, Bureau of Economics and Statistics, Registrar of Cooperative Societies, financial institutions and GIC etc. SLCCCI notifies the crops and areas to be covered during the season. State Government submits the yield data for premium calculation and also at the time of harvest yield data based on crop cutting experiments (CCEs) conducted by State machinery based on which claims are worked out. State machinery also helps in publicity.

Proposals are received and processed by the banks– commercial banks, regional rural banks, cooperative banks etc. Nodal offices of the banks are decided at the time of notification depending on the infrastructure available in particular areas. Farmers interested for taking insurance open bank accounts and submit proposal forms. Banks submit consolidated crop insurance declarations on monthly basis along with premium to the State Level Offices of the implementing agency who underwrite business. Claim payments are also made through the banks concerned who credit the claim amount in the bank account of the individual farmer.

The premium rates are 3.5 per cent (of sum insured) for bajra and oilseeds, 2.5 per cent for other kharif crops, 1.5 per cent for wheat, and 2 per cent for other Rabi crops, while actuarial rates are being charged in the case of commercial/horticultural crops. Small and marginal farmers are entitled to a subsidy of 50 per cent of the premium, which is shared on 50:50 basis by the Central and State Governments. The premium subsidy will be phased out over period of 5 years. At present, the scheme is being implemented by 21 States and 2 Union Territories.

5.4.2 Rainfall Insurance Scheme *Varsha Bima:* AICIL introduced Rainfall Insurance Scheme known as *Varsha Bima* during 2004 south-west monsoon period. *Varsha Bima* provided for the following five different options suiting varied requirements of farming community.

- Seasonal rainfall insurance based on aggregated rainfall from June to September.
- Sowing failure insurance based on rainfall between June 15 and August 15.
- Rainfall distribution insurance with the weight assigned to different weeks between June and September.
- Agronomic index constructed on the basis of water requirements of crops.
- A catastrophe option covering extremely adverse deviation of 50 per cent and above in rainfall during the season.

Varsha Bima was piloted in 20 rain-gauge areas spread over Andhra Pradesh, Karnataka, Rajasthan and Uttar Pradesh in 2004-05.

Based on the experience of the pilot project, the scheme was fine-tuned and implemented as *Varsha Bima-2005* in around 130 districts across Andhra Pradesh, Chhatisgarh, Gujarat, Karnataka, Maharashtra, Madhya Pradesh, Orissa, Tamil Nadu, Uttarakhand and Uttar Pradesh during kharif 2005.

During kharif 2006, the scheme was implemented as *Varsha Bima-2006* in and around 150 districts/rain gauge station areas covering 16 states across the country. AICIL is also piloting another weather related insurance product for mango and coffee.

5.5 Other Initiatives

5.5.1 Pilot Scheme on Seed Crop Insurance: In addition to National Agricultural Insurance Scheme (NAIS), the Government of India introduced a Central Sector "Pilot Scheme on Seed Crop Insurance (PSSCI)" from Rabi 1999-2000 season covering breeder seeds, foundation seeds and certified seeds of all major crops in 10 States. It is a path-breaking scheme introduced for the first time to provide financial security and income stability to the seed growers, stimulate seed production of newly release varieties and to give boost to the modern seed industry. The scheme shall cover losses both at field stage and seed certification stage. It is a commercial scheme to be implemented on sound insurance principles.

PSSCI covers seed crops of paddy, wheat, maize, jowar, bajra, gram, red gram, groundnut, soybean, sunflower and cotton. The scheme covers seed crop at field stage arising out of failure, rejection of seed crop, loss in expected raw seed yield and loss of seed crop after the harvest. It also covers germination losses at the certification stage. Most of the non-preventable natural risks such as flood, fire, storm, drought, excessive rain, incidence of pests and diseases etc. have been covered. The sum insured is equivalent to preceding three or five years average seed yield multiplied by procurement price/sale price of seed crop. The premium rates are 2 per cent for wheat and groundnut, 2.5 per cent for sunflower, 3 per cent for paddy, 3.5 per cent for jowar and 5 per cent for gram, red gram, bajara, maize, soybean and cotton. Premium and claims up to 200 per cent of premium will be met by the Government of India on sunset basis - first year – 100 per cent, second year 50 per cent and third year 25 per cent.

5.5.2 Farm Income Insurance Scheme (FIIS): In order

to target the two critical components of a farmer's income, namely yield and price, through a single policy instrument, the Department of Agriculture & Cooperation formulated the Farm Income Insurance Scheme (FIIS). This Scheme was conceived to provide income protection to the farmers by integrating the mechanism of insuring production as well as market risks. Initially the scheme was taken up on a pilot basis during *rabi* season 2003-04 in 18 districts of 12 States for wheat and paddy. Based on the outcome of the pilot implementation, the scheme would be appropriately fine-tuned as necessary. Main features of FIIS are the following.

- Farmers will be protected by ensuring minimum guaranteed income.
- If the actual income of the farmers falls short of the guaranteed income (product of average yield and MSP) of the farmers they would be eligible for compensation to the extent of indemnity from the Agriculture Insurance Company of India Ltd. (AICI).
- Area approach as in NAIS would be used for actual yield and price measurement of the insured crop.
- Initially the scheme would cover paddy and wheat only.
- The scheme would be available for all the States and would be compulsory for farmers availing crop loans.
- NAIS will be withdrawn for the crops covered under FIIS but would continue to be applicable for other crops.

5.5.3 Livestock Insurance: Livestock Insurance business consisting mainly of Cattle Insurance is being implemented by the following four public sector general insurance companies.

- National Insurance Community Ltd.
- New India Assurance Community Ltd.
- Oriental Insurance Community Ltd.
- United India Insurance Community Ltd.

Under the various Livestock Insurance Policies, cover is provided for the sum insured or the market value of the animal at the time of death, whichever is less. Animals are insured up to 100 percent of their market value normally.

Cattle insurance scheme commenced in 1974 in the country. It covers cows, buffaloes, calves, bulls etc. The cattle have been classified under two categories - scheme and non-scheme. Scheme animals are those which are financed and/or subsidised under Central/State Government schemes.

5.5.4 Non-crop Insurance Schemes: In additional to crop insurance scheme, several non- crop insurance schemes have also been introduced in the country. Some of the important non-crop insurance schemes are the following.

- Pilot Scheme on Seed Crop Insurance (PSSCI).
- Cattle insurance.
- Poultry/duck/quail insurance.
- Horticulture/plantation insurance.
- Floriculture insurance.
- Aqua-culture insurance.
- Sericulture insurance.
- Honey bee insurance.
- Agriculture pump-set insurance.

5.5.5 Agriculture Insurance Corporation: Union Budget 2002-03 proposed setting up of a separate Corporation for Agriculture Insurance to be promoted by the existing public sector general insurance companies. A Task Force was constituted to oversee the setting up of the Agriculture Insurance Corporation. It was decided by the Task Force that the new company will be named as 'Agriculture Insurance Company of India Ltd.' and will be registered under the Companies Act, 1956 with the capital participation from General Insurance Corporation of India (GIC), four public sector general insurance companies, viz. National Insurance Community Ltd., New India Assurance Community Ltd., Oriental Insurance Community Ltd. and United India Insurance Community Ltd. and NABARD.

The promoters' subscription to the paid-up capital will be 35 per cent by GIC, 30 percent by NABARD and 8.75 per cent each by the four public sector general insurance companies. The authorised capital of the new organization will be Rs.

1500 crore, while the initial paid-up capital will be Rs. 200 crore. National Agriculture Insurance Scheme (NAIS) shall be transferred to the new organization and shall form the core of business to begin with. Transition to actuarial regime will be made over a period of time. The new organization will, in due course, cover other allied rural/agricultural risks in addition to crop insurance.

The Registrar of Companies (Delhi & Haryana) has approved the name of the new company as Agriculture Insurance Company of India Ltd. The new company has since been incorporated under the Companies Act, 1956 on 20.12.2002.

5.5.6 R.N. Malhotra Committee (1994) on Rural Insurance: The Committee on Reforms in the Insurance Sector (Chairman: R.N. Malhotra) which submitted its report in January 1994 made the following recommendations pertaining to rural insurance.

- There is need for more intensive work in rural areas for spreading non-traditional insurance business. For this purpose, help may be taken from panchayats, co-operatives and NGOs.
- The new entrants may be required to undertake a specified proportion of their business as rural non-traditional business.
- Request from the co-operative institutions to transact general insurance business may be considered favourably.
- Welfare oriented schemes such as Pass and Hut should be transferred to concerned government authorities.

5.5.6 Summing Up: The insurance companies which have confined their business operations to urban sector and plan to enter in agriculture sector may have to chalk out specific strategy and policy package for the same. The main elements of the strategy could be as under.

First, the insurance products designed for agriculture sector should be as simple as possible and in non-legal and non technical terminology. Most of the farmers are illiterate and ignorant and have not been exposed to insurance services. They have to be convinced about the benefits flowing from insurance covers. It may be difficult to market highly technical and complicated products in the agriculture sector. These covers should easily be understandable by the farmers. In order to gain a foothold in the agriculture sector, insurance companies may prefer to introduce some of the existing popular products with suitable modifications as to meet the requirements of rural sector. Once a beginning has been made and farmers get used to insurance services and are convinced about its benefits, technically strong products may be introduced. In the beginning companies may introduce non-crop products such as cattle insurance which can easily be administered and are also easily understood by rural population. Thereafter, products directly related with agriculture may be introduced.

Second, to the extent possible, package approach to insurance products may be adopted. In the agriculture sector, farmers are exposed to several risks and instead of designing several individual covers for these risks, it would be a good marketing strategy to formulate package covers, incorporating different risks in a single policy. It would enhance saleability of these products. However, these companies have to be careful to see that package covers are properly designed and not simply combination of individual policies so as to make them complicated and ambiguous.

Third, insurance companies should make all the efforts and initiate appropriate measures to bring down the administrative costs of agriculture insurance business. The delivery and servicing cost of insurance products in agriculture sector is quite high on the one hand, while premium per policy is low on the other. One of the policy measures may be to have a liaison with banking institutions which may have created infrastructure in rural sector and might be having efficient marketing network. A close co-operation with banking sector will help insurance companies to reduce and minimise their overhead cost. The co-operation may also be sought from local agencies such as Co-operatives, Panchayats, Marketing Boards etc. for marketing the products. These agencies could function as marketing agents for insurance companies and suitable agency commission and incentives may be devised for them.

Similar to group life policies for industrial workers in urban sector which are purchased by the employer, in agriculture sector also, master policies may be designed and sold to some nodal agency who will be responsible for collection of premium from farmers, informing them about the coverage of their risks and also processing their claim papers. For controlling the cost, insurance companies instead of commencing their business simultaneously in all the areas of the country, may initially start operations in few selected areas based upon potentiality study. Based upon the experience and after establishing basic organisational infrastructure, these companies may gradually extend operations in other areas.

Appendices

Appendix 1

Edited Extracts from Eleventh Five Year Plan (2007-12) on Agricultural Credit

---

Agricultural Credit

Credit is an essential requirement for revitalising agriculture and there have been some important positive developments in this area. The total credit to agriculture increased from Rs. 62,045 crore during 2001-02, the terminal year of the Ninth Five-Year Plan to Rs. 2,00,000 crore during 2006-07, the final year of the Tenth Five-Year Plan. This was a more than three fold increase over five years. The share of Commercial Banks in total agricultural credit increased from 54 per cent in 2001-02 to around 69 cent in 2005-06. The share of investment credit increased from 35 per cent in 2001-02 to around 41 per cent in 2004-05, despite the negative growth achieved by the long term cooperative credit structure. As against a target of Rs. 7,36,570 crore, the total institutional credit flow to agriculture during the Tenth Five-Year Plan is expected to be above Rs. 6,50,000 crore, i.e. a likely compound annual growth rate (CAGR) of 26 per cent . This is much better than the CAGR of 18% achieved during the Ninth Five Year Plan.

The growth of credit was especially impressive during the last two years of the Tenth Plan on account of the "Farm Credit Package" announced by the Government of India (GoI). A Special 'Farm Credit Package' as enunciated by the GoI on 18 June 2005 for doubling the credit flow to agriculture, contained various innovative propositions for credit growth. As per provisional figures available for 2005-06, the ground level credit flow to agriculture during 2005-06 was Rs. 1,80,446 crore; 128 per cent of the target of Rs. 1,41,000 crore, and registering an annual growth of 44 per cent. While Commercial Banks registered a growth of 54 per cent during the year, Cooperative Banks recorded 25 per cent growth, followed by Regional Rural Banks at 22 per cent.

However, although the total agricultural credit has increased during the Tenth Plan period, there are serious quantitative as well as qualitative concerns. The outreach of the formal institutional credit structure is very limited. The findings of the National Sample Survey Organization (NSSO) 59th Round (2003), revealed that only 27 per cent of the total number of cultivator households received credit from formal sources while 22 per cent received credit from informal sources. The remaining households, comprising mainly small and marginal farmers, had no credit outstanding. It is unlikely that the situation has changed much since 2003.

Comprehensive measures aimed at financial inclusion in terms of innovative products and services to increase access to institutional credit are urgently required. Issues such as credit flow to tenant farmers, oral lessees and women cultivators, complex documentation processes, high transaction costs, inadequate and ineffective risk mitigation arrangements, poor extension services, weak marketing links and sectoral and regional issues in credit are also required to be addressed expeditiously. The agrarian crisis also led to default by many farmers, and a consequent freeze on their ability to access institutional credit. The overhang of such nonperforming debt also needs to be reduced.

The share of direct accounts with a credit limit of less than Rs. 25,000 in total direct accounts declined from 97 per cent in 1990 to 67 per cent in 2005, while their share in direct credit has declined precipitously. The coverage of operational holdings needs to be increased significantly, with sub-targets for the less developed states and small and marginal farmers. Considering that for small and marginal farmers the only alternate sources of finance are expensive loans from moneylenders, the share of direct accounts with a credit limit of Rs. 25,000 in total direct finance may be targeted at a substantially higher level.

At present direct finance to agriculture under priority sector lending includes credit for the purchase of trucks, mini-trucks, jeeps, pick- up vans, bullock carts and other transport equipment to assist the transport of agricultural inputs and farm produce. Direct finance also includes credit for the construction and running of cold storage facilities, warehouses and godowns. As alternate formal sources of finance are available for these activities, their inclusion under direct finance for agriculture needs to be reconsidered.

Special credit packages with varying and flexible repayment periods may be thought of for the agriculture sector to take care of mismatches of income and expenditure flows of farmers and the seasonal nature of agricultural income. Doorstep banking implemented through designated agent of commercial banks has now been facilitated by decent decision of the Reserve Bank of India and provides an opportunity for farmers to interact with banks with timings suitable to the farming community. The banks are currently allowed to extend financial outreach by utilising the services of civil society organisations, Farmers' Clubs, NGOs, Post Offices etc. as "Business Facilitators" or as "Business Correspondents". NABARD could look into the reasons which are coming in the way of the banks using intermediaries as facilitators/ correspondents and approach RBI for necessary changes/ amendments in the instructions on the subject.

Cooperatives

The credit disbursal by commercial banks covers only 11.7 per cent of operational holdings in the country. Credit growth by the cooperatives to the agriculture sector has gradually picked up during the course of the Tenth Five Year Plan. The number of loan accounts have, however declined from 224.6 lakh in 2004-05 to 192.8 lakh in 2005-06. The most potent means *for widening and deepening access to institutional* credit to the innumerable small and marginal farmers are the Co-operative Credit Societies that are autonomous and democratic. The revitalisation of the cooperative credit structure in order to transform them into vibrant and viable democratic financial institutions is therefore vital. It is, therefore, extremely important, that the restructuring of cooperative credit now in progress, on the lines of the recommendations of A. Vaidyanathan Committee are implemented speedily and rigorously. MoUs have been signed by 13 State Governments and the process of auditing of accounts is under way. It is necessary to move quickly to take the next steps in depoliticising the system.

Risk Management

The frequency and severity of risks in agriculture particularly in last few decades has increased on account of climate variability. The principal evidence of climatic change has been rising temperatures, erratic rainfall pattern, and increase in the severity of droughts, floods and cyclones which have caused huge losses in agricultural production and the livestock population. India has developed response mechanisms for primary (crop failures) and to some extent secondary (livestock deaths) consequences of climate variability. However, a tertiary mechanism which goes beyond resource transfer to resource assessment and management, through climate forecasting, climate information generation and dissemination, early warning system, mapping of agricultural losses through remote sensing technology and a pre and post climate change response need to be put in place on a decentralized basis. Such a response mechanism must include putting in place a catastrophe protection insurance mechanism as also provision of bankruptcy legislation for the farmers.

Crop insurance was introduced in the country two decades ago. The present version, the **National Agricultural Insurance Scheme** (NAIS) is available since 1999-2000. Despite States' support for coverage of the NAIS being tardy, NAIS is a useful device, especially for farmers growing relatively risky crops. The main problem is that NAIS is not really actuarial insurance. Premiums for most important crops are fixed at All-India level irrespective of risk and government pays for entire excess of claims over premium received. Moreover, being compulsory for all borrowers from banks in States where it is in force, and with relatively few non-loanee farmers involved, it mainly insures banks against default following poor harvest. Further, its popularity with farmers is limited since it is based on crop-cutting experiments, which delays claims payments till well after harvest and the risk covered is only of yield shortfalls at the block level. There is a scope for improving the coverage of NAIS in terms of regions and crops, substitution of long term yield rate as a bench mark and ensuring prompt payment of the indemnities. Decision to devolve the area of damage assessment from blocks to smaller units may be done with care, as the costs of such decentralization and the moral hazards will be very high compared to the likely benefits. Other indicators, such as rainfall, could be used for assessing the damage due to natural factors. Some States are devising their own crop insurance policies including weather insurance, which can be supported in suitable ways. However, for the next few years they should not be treated as a substitute to NAIS.

An important lacuna, which many researchers have pointed out, is the rather indifferent attitude of the banks towards crop insurance. All commercial banks, RRBs and the Cooperative Banks should make crop insurance mandatory for all agricultural loanees, especially because such insurance can indirectly contribute to the viability of rural banking. An equally important aspect is the need for much larger involvement of the states in the functioning of the scheme. Government needs to take up agricultural reinsurance more extensively with appropriate insurance products. Recently some of the successful insurance products like Rainfall Insurance have been developed by ICICI-Lombard General Insurance Company and by IFFCO-Tokyo General Insurance

Company. Under the scheme coverage for deviation in rainfall index is extended and compensations for economic losses due to the less or more than normal rainfall are paid. There is a lot of interest in private sector for insurance business. Necessary incentives should be devised for insurance companies to design suitable products for agriculture sector

Appendix 2

Recommendations of the Committee on Financial Inclusion (Chairman: C. Rangarajan), January 2008

Early Implementation of Vaidyanathan Committee Revival Package

All necessary steps should be taken for the early implementation of the STCCS revival package in all States.

Cooperatives in SHG-Bank Linkage: Need for Enabling Legislation

In certain States, legislation has been enacted, admitting SHGs as members of PACS. Similar legislation in other States would require to be enacted to enable the emergence of cooperatives as effective SHPIs. Federations of SHGs may be registered in all the States under the Cooperative Societies Act or the parallel Self Reliant Cooperatives Act and availability of funds to these cooperatives for advancing loans may be considered by NABARD, based on objective rating criteria. NABARD may also set aside requisite funds for sensitising the cooperative movement in this regard.

Use of PACS and other Primary Cooperatives as Business Correspondents

There are a large number of PACS and primary cooperatives under the parallel Acts located in rural areas where there are no other financial services outlets. Many of these cooperatives are in districts where the DCCBs are defunct or moribund. Such PACS could provide valuable services to their members if they get access to a commercial bank. RBI has already listed Cooperatives as eligible institutions under the BF/BC Model.

In the circumstances, Cooperatives may make use of this

opportunity at least in States which have accepted the Vaidyanathan Committee recommendations. NABARD may be asked to suggest appropriate guidelines for the purpose, subject to the approval of RBI.

Cooperatives Adopting Group Approach for Financing Excluded Groups

Micro-enterprises, in order to be successful, require larger funding which NGOs cannot provide. It will, therefore, be necessary to develop / test a new form of community based organisation other than SHGs which may be more appropriate to support members who engage in micro-enterprises. Those members of SHG who opt to graduate to micro-enterprises could be formed into JLGs or some similar organisation.

The relations of mutual trust and support which is described as affinity in a SHG tend to be weaker in a JLG. Therefore, new forms of collateral or guarantee may have to be worked out. Guidelines circulated by NABARD may be adopted by banks.

Further, the use of the BF model could be thought of to organize vulnerable segments of the population into JLGs. The pilot project presently under implementation by NABARD should be sufficiently broad based to cover the role of facilitators in formation and linkage of JLGs.

Risk Mitigation: Setting up of Credit Guarantee Fund

A Credit Guarantee Fund may be set up as a risk mitigation mechanism and also for providing comfort to the banks for lending to such JLGs (akin to the Credit Guarantee Fund Scheme of SIDBI for Small/Micro enterprises Industries - CGFSI - available for small-scale industries - SSI - at present).

Self Help Group–Bank Linkage Model

The SHG-Bank Linkage Programme is a major plank of the strategy for delivering financial services to the poor in a sustainable manner. As at the end of March 2007, as many as

29.25 lakh SHGs have been credit-linked with banks, benefiting more than 400 lakh poor families. There is a need for further deepening and upscaling of microfinance interventions.

Encouraging SHGs in Excluded Regions: Funding Support

If the SHG-Bank Linkage programme has to reach a critical scale, the Department of Women and Child Development at State-level should be actively involved in promoting and nurturing of SHGs. The State Govts. and NABARD may, therefore, set aside specific funds out of budgetary support and the Micro Finance Development and Equity Fund (MFDEF) respectively for the purpose of promoting SHGs in regions with high levels of exclusion.

The spread of SHGs in hilly regions, particularly in the North-Eastern Region, is poor. One of the reasons for this is the low population density in hilly areas and weak banking network. There is a need to evolve SHG models suited to the local context.

Capacity Building of Government Functionaries

Certain deficiencies like poor follow up, ineffective monitoring and inadequate training and capacity building efforts have been observed in the past. Adequate safeguards may, therefore, be devised and built in future programme implementation strategies. NABARD can also facilitate this process by providing support for capacity building of Government functionaries from grass root level upwards within the SHG framework.

Legal Status for SHGs

As of now, SHGs are operating as thrift and credit groups. They may, in future, evolve to a higher level of commercial enterprise. The question of providing a simplified legal status to the SHGs may have to be examined in full, in this context. This would also facilitate their becoming members of PACS.

Maintenance of Participatory Character of SHG Movement

A movement of such large scale involving people's participation could lead to attempts towards politicization. This must be avoided. Sufficient care has to be taken to ensure that the SHG movement retains its participatory and self-help character.

NABARD to Open 'Project Offices' in Identified Priority States

NABARD is managing the MFDEF with a corpus of Rs. 200 crore. One major focus of the Fund should be promoting the SHG-Bank Linkage Programme in States where it has been comparatively slow moving. NABARD has already identified States with large population of the poor, but exhibiting low performance in implementation of the programme. The ongoing efforts of NABARD to upscale the programme in the identified States need to be given a fresh impetus.

NABARD can open dedicated project offices in the 13 States for upscaling the SHG - Bank Linkage Programme by strategizing interventions such as stronger involvement of State Governments, capacity building of NGOs, broadening the range of SHPI, etc.

Incentive Package for NGOs

Many of the NGOs have played a commendable role in promoting SHGs and linking them with banks. NGOs, being local initiators with their low resources are finding it difficult to expand in other areas and regions. There is, therefore, a need to evolve an incentive package which should motivate these NGOs to diversify into other backward areas. Incentive package could be in the form of expeditious and hassle-free grant support.

RBI/NABARD to Study the Issue of 'Evergreening'

A certain element of "evergreening" of loans is reportedly

taking place among credit linked SHGs. This, if established, is a matter of concern. RBI/ NABARD may expeditiously study this aspect and come out with suggestions for reversing this unsettling trend.

Transparency in Maintenance of Records

In order to ensure sustainability of the SHGs, their activities and linkages, there should be better transparency in the books of accounts maintained at the group level. These books should reflect the position of deposits in members' accounts, interest paid on savings, distribution of corpus or operating surplus among members, evergreening of loan accounts, etc. Banks, with the help of NABARD, should evolve a checklist for concurrent monitoring of SHGs.

SHGs to Evolve Norms for Distribution of Surplus

Many of the SHGs do not have the practice of distributing the surplus generated from their business activities within the group and the awareness on this issue among the SHG members is very low. There is a need to evolve norms for distribution of surplus (akin to dividend) especially at the time when a member drops out of the group.

Need to Restructure Design & Direction of SGSY Subsidy

Subsidies provided under SGSY need to be restructured. Linking credit with subsidy is not an effective approach for reaching out to the poor. There is a need to formulate a single programme synergising the positive features of SGSY such as specific targeting of Below Poverty Line (BPL) families, etc. and those of the SHG – Bank Linkage Programme such as group cohesiveness, discipline etc.

While recognizing that individual subsidies are distortionary, the Government may consider redirecting subsidy in the SGSY Programme for the following purposes:

- Capacity building of NGOs and other field based agencies such as Krishi Vigyan Kendras, to form and strengthen

SHGs.

- Exposure visits to successful models by bankers, government officials and SHG leaders etc.
- For strengthening input supply and marketing arrangements.

Some of the State Governments like West Bengal and Andhra Pradesh have initiated efforts in this direction. Further, it is understood that the proposals are awaiting approval of the GoI. The approaches adopted by these States for bringing synergy between SGSY groups and the SHGs of the linkage programme can be studied so that the same can be replicated in other States. The broad features of the proposed convergence model are indicated in Annexure V of the main report.

The need for technology adoption for effective disbursal of Govt. subsidy should be recognized. The existing dispensation of subsidy under SGSY and payouts under NREGP could be routed thru' bank accounts, with suitable technology support.

Interest Rate Subsidy

Certain States are reportedly providing a subsidy on interest rates being charged by banks to the SHGs. The margin available to SHGs is sufficient to take care of operational costs, even after considering the small amounts of loan provided to members. Thus, a subsidy on interest rates cuts at the very root of the self help character of SHGs. The subsidy could be re-directed towards capacity building efforts or in providing input supplies and marketing support to the SHGs.

Resource Centres

For ensuring the long term sustainability of SHGs and for helping the members of mature SHGs to graduate from microfinance to micro-enterprises, Resource Centres on the lines of the Andhra Pradesh Mahila Abhivruddhi Society (APMAS) can be set up in different parts of the country.

There are a large number of SHGs which are well established in their savings and credit operations. Their members want to expand and diversify their activities with a view to attain economies of scale. Many of the groups are organizing themselves into federations and other higher level structures. To achieve this effectively, resource centres can play a vital role.

Resource centres can be set up by various stakeholders such as NGOs, banks, Government departments, NABARD at the State/district level to play an important role in preparing training modules, developing a cadre of trainers, conduct of field studies and in promoting interface between SHG members and service providers. The specific role of Resource Centres would be :

- To work towards a comprehensive capacity building of SHGs,
- Share innovative ideas and models that can be replicated elsewhere,
- Enhance functional literacy among SHG members,
- Support livelihood interventions among SHG members,
- Facilitate availability of all services to SHG members under one roof.

The cost for setting up Resource Centres can be met out of the Financial Inclusion Fund and/or the MFDEF.

SHGs to Provide Alternative Savings Products

Most of the SHGs encourage compulsory savings with equal small amounts by members on a regular basis. SHGs need to offer a wide range of savings products so as to capture the huge potential of savings that remains untapped. Groups should be free to design savings products suiting to members' requirements. Certain level of experimentation could be attempted by the Resource Centres in designing new saving products and NABARD should encourage and support such experiments.

Adoption of JLG Model to Cover Marginalized Groups

A scheme for financing JLGs of tenant farmers and oral

lessees has been evolved by NABARD for implementation by all the commercial banks, RRBs and Cooperatives. The adoption of the concept of JLGs, if properly grounded, could be another effective method for purveying credit to mid-segment clients such as small farmers, marginal farmers, tenant farmers, etc. and thereby reduce their dependence on informal sources of credit.

From Microcredit to Microenterprise: Challenges

The present challenge is to induce SHGs and their members to graduate into matured levels of enterprise, factor in livelihood diversification, increase their access to the supply chain, linkages to the capital market and appropriate production and processing technologies.

A spin off of this challenge is how to address the investment capital requirements of matured SHGs, which have initially met members' consumption needs and are now on the threshold of taking off into "enterprise". There is evidence in MYRADA experience where lending for productive purposes has already been given greater emphasis by SHGs. The Community Managed Resource Centres (CMRCs) organized by MYRADA provide a variety of linkage services to SHGs and individual entrepreneurs among SHG members. This model requires to be studied.

The SHG - Bank Linkage Programme needs to introspect whether it is sufficient for SHGs to only meet the financial needs of their members, or whether there is also a further obligation on their part to meet the non-financial requirements necessary for setting up business and enterprises. Ideally, it must meet both.

Greater Role for NABARD

While greater emphasis is needed for growth and spread of SHGs across the country, the quality in terms of outreach of financial services, capacity building, sustainability etc., needs to be reemphasized. NABARD shall play a pro-active role and identify new initiatives that will contribute to effectively improving outreach to the poor thru' SHGs, MFIs etc.

Federations

Federations, if they emerge voluntarily from amongst SHGs, can be encouraged. However, the Committee feels that they cannot be entrusted with the financial intermediation function. In Andhra Pradesh, federations are registered as societies under the MACS Act. The SHG members (as individuals) are permitted to be members in the federation. In Uttarakhand, SHGs are permitted to become members of PACS directly. Other States may adopt similar enabling legislation.

Voluntary establishment of federations could be supported out of the Financial Inclusion Fund and the MFDEF. While extending support, it should be ensured that:

- Federations emerge voluntarily, on the felt need of the SHGs,
- Federations provide other value added services to member SHGs. Based on a study of Federations operating across the country, a broad list of such services and the modus operandi of federations in providing such services can be prepared and circulated by NABARD.
- Federations, in terms of distance, operate in close proximity to members.

Urban Microfinance

There are no clear estimates of the number of people in urban areas with no access to organized financial services. This may be attributed, in part at least, to the migratory nature of the urban poor, comprising mostly of migrants from the rural areas. Even money lenders often shy away from lending to urban poor.

There have been a few instances of MFIs venturing into this area of lending to urban poor who are undertaking micro-enterprises and small business activities. Urban branches of banks, even though having manpower and technology support, are not attuned to SHG lending or microfinance.

Opening of specialised microfinance branches / cells in potential urban centers exclusively catering for microfinance and SHG - bank linkages could be thought of, to address the requirements of the urban poor. BFs / BCs could be the mechanism to reach the target clientele in these areas. Banks can also consider associating with MFIs undertaking urban microlending as a viable option.

Amendment to NABARD Act

At present, NABARD is permitted, as per its Act and Mandate, to support micro finance activities in rural and semi-urban areas only. An enabling provision be made in the NABARD Act, 1981 permitting NABARD to provide micro finance services to the urban poor.

Micro Finance Institutions: Introduction

Firm data regarding the number of MFIs operating under different forms is not available. However, it is roughly estimated that there are about 1,000 NGO-MFIs and more than 20 Company MFIs. Further, in Andhra Pradesh, nearly 30,000 cooperative organizations are engaged in mF activities. However, the company MFIs are major players accounting for over 80% of the micro finance loan portfolio.

Definition of MFI

The proposed Microfinance Services Regulation Bill defines microfinance services as “providing financial assistance to an individual or an eligible client, either directly or through a group mechanism for an amount, not exceeding rupees fifty thousand in aggregate (Rs.1,50,000 if for housing purposes)

Greater legitimacy, accountability and transparency will not only enable MFIs to source adequate debt and equity funds, but could eventually enable MFIs to take and use savings as a low cost source for on-lending.

Recognising MF-NBFCs

There is a need to recognize a separate category of Micro finance – Non-banking Finance Companies (MF–NBFCs), without any relaxation on start-up capital and subject to the regulatory prescriptions applicable for NBFCs. Such MF-NBFCs could be defined as companies that provide thrift, credit, micro-insurance, remittances and other financial services up to a specified amount to the poor in rural, semi-urban and urban areas.

At least 80% of the assets of MF-NBFCs should be in the form of microcredit of up to Rs. 50,000 for agriculture, allied and non farm activities and in case of housing, loans up to Rs. 1,50,000 per individual borrower, whether given through a group mechanism or directly.

MF-NBFCs as BCs

To enable the poor to have access to savings services, MF-NBFCs may be recognized as Business Correspondents of banks for only providing savings and remittance services.

Relaxation in FIPB guidelines

Current guidelines used by FIPB (Foreign Investment Promotion Board) require a minimum of US$ 500,000 equity investment from a foreign entity. MFNBFCs' initial capital needs may not be very large and the Committee is of the view that the minimum amount of foreign equity for MF-NBFCs may be reduced to a level of US$ 100,000.

NABARD may extend equity support out of its MFDEF to such MF-NBFCs based on objective rating/criteria. NABARD may accord priority in providing equity support to those MF-NBFCs operating in regions featuring high levels of exclusion.

The SEBI Venture Capital Guidelines may permit Venture Capital Funds to invest in MF-NBFCs.

Tax Concessions

MF-NBFCs may be allowed tax concessions to the extent of 40% of their profits, as a proportion to their business portfolio in excluded districts as identified by NABARD without attracting tax. For this, MF-NBFCs may be included as eligible institutions under Section 36(1) (viii) of the Income Tax Act.

MF-NBFCs as Microinsurance Agents

The IRDA Microinsurance Guidelines, 2005 may permit MF-NBFCs to offer microinsurance services as agents of regulated life and non-life insurance companies.

Code of Conduct

A voluntary mutual code of conduct, already prepared, covering aspects including mission, governance, transparency, interest rates, handling of customer grievances, staff conduct, recovery practices, etc., may be made mandatory for MFIs.

Accounting and Disclosure Norms

The Institute of Chartered Accountants of India (ICAI) may be involved in formulating appropriate accounting and disclosure norms for MFIs.

Banks lending to MFIs may undertake studies on the cost of funds of MFIs, risk premium, etc. and exercise a lender's discipline in enforcing reasonable rates of interest and acceptable modes of recovery.

Unifying Regulatory Oversight

RBI may consider bringing all regulatory aspects of microfinance under a single mechanism. Further, supervision of MF-NBFCs could be delegated to NABARD by RBI.

Micro Finance Bill

While Section 25 Companies could be covered by the Micro Financial Sector (Development and Regulation) Bill,

2007, cooperatives can be taken out of the purview of the proposed Bill.

Technology Applications

Technology: The Driving Force for Low-cost Inclusion Initiatives

Technological developments in the recent past have provided the perfect launch pad for extending banking outposts to remote locations without having to open bank branches. This could be achieved by leveraging technology to open up channels beyond branch network and create the required banking footprints to reach the unbanked so as to extend banking services similar to those dispensed from branches.

The Committee, while concurring with the RBI's advisory group for ITenabled financial inclusion, is of the view that nearly all pilot models converge on certain essential components and processes to be followed in technology application. The essence of a majority of the models under consideration features the issue of a smart card to the farmer on which all his transactions are recorded, a hand-held terminal with the BC at the village level and a Central Processor Unit (CPU) linking the smart cards and BC terminals with the banks. There are also other models where smart cards are dispensed with and mobile telephones, etc., are used.

The fundamental outlines of the existing technology-based models may be examined for application in such manner and to such extent as may be deemed fit.

The operating costs of the various models are expected to be minimal and can be easily absorbed by banks as the increase in business volumes will justify the incremental operating costs. Also, the costs are substantially lowered if the infrastructure is shared. It is, therefore, recommended that shared infrastructure among different banks enabling nationwide financial inclusion would confer large scale benefits and also enable effortless transfer of funds between the card holders of various banks.

Essentially, the start up costs are the initial investment costs comprising cost of the smart card, terminals with the BC and the CPU. The Committee is of the view that the Financial Inclusion Technology Fund can provide the necessary support for defraying part of the costs.

Optimisation of Existing Infrastructure

The Committee is of the opinion that the existing banking infra-structure and NGOs which have already made extensive inroads in rural areas should be made optimal use of for enabling outreach of banking services. The BF/BC models backed by technology applications should encourage a role for the small players and integrate them with the national system. The Committee is of the opinion that the State Governments should make payments under National Rural Employment Guarantee Scheme and Social Security Payments thru' such technology based solutions.

Building Database

The creation of a national data-base, sectoral, geographic and demographic reports, and also a payment system benefiting the card holders from the underprivileged/unbanked population will not be possible without the extensive use of IT. This alone can bring down the costs of the small ticket transactions of the poor and make nationwide financial inclusion a reality. The technology suppliers and banks should evolve common minimum standards for ensuring inter-operability between their systems.

Remittance Needs of Poor

Ahmednagar DCCB has implemented a system of low cost anywhere banking solution which has a facility of card to card transfer. Savings/current account holders at all its 280 branches have a choice to keep their savings bank account or a part thereof in a separate account at the bank's head office.

Customers can have access to this account from all the bank branches. It was learnt that the customer is charged only Rs. 4 per transaction. Such experiments may be studied for replication.

A low value card linked to a bank account, which can be encashed at PoS and which allow transfer of small amounts from one card to another would alleviate remittance problems. This would substantially increase banking outreach as at present there are about 3 lakh PoS as compared to around 70,000 scheduled commercial bank branches and 22,000 ATMs. However, a majority of PoS machines are now located in urban and semi-urban areas. It is expected that as the system takes roots, more PoS will come in rural areas, facilitating such transfers.

The e-kiosks in villages could be yet another source of operating a remittance system that is accessible to the poor.

Other Recommendations

The following suggestions would substantially address the remittance needs of the poor in the country:

- The combined network of nearly 70000 branches of scheduled commercial banks (including RRBs) and a network of more than 1.50 lakh post offices can ideally provide the institutional mechanism for extending remittance facilities in remote areas. With adoption of appropriate technology, it may be possible to bring down the transaction costs which would encourage and enable the poor to make use of such remittance facilities. A committee may be set up with representatives from RBI, Department of Posts, NABARD and commercial banks for exploring the feasibility of integrating postal network with the banking system and developing a nation wide remittance system.
- The remittance product could be an electronic product similar to "Instacash" where a 16 digit code is given to the originator of the transaction, and the beneficiary can take

the amount from select post offices by giving the code, and identity proof. This product should be available across banks, post offices and other institutions and be affordable. Another option could be to credit the remitted amount to a central server at the originating point and at every touch point should be able to withdraw it.

- Banks should endeavour to have a BC touch point in each of the six lakh villages in the country. There should be a micro-bank in every village.
- Banks should introduce card-based remittance products which can be encashed all over the country. This may be card to card transfer, or simply a scratch card type remittance card.

Micro Insurance

Micro-insurance should provide greater economic and psychological security to the poor as it reduces exposure to multiple risks and cushions the impact of a disaster. Micro-insurance in conjunction with micro savings and micro credit could go a long way in keeping this segment away from the poverty trap and would truly be an integral component of financial inclusion.

In 2003, GoI constituted a Consultative Group on Micro-Insurance to examine existing insurance schemes for rural and urban poor. The report of the consultative group has brought out the following key issues:

- Micro-insurance is not viable as a standalone insurance product.
- Micro-insurance has not penetrated rural markets. Traditional insurers have not made much headway in bringing micro-insurance products to the rural poor. (In addition, the Committee feels that micro insurance has not penetrated even among the urban poor).
- Partnership between an insurer and a social organisation like NGO would be desirable to promote micro-insurance by drawing on their mutual strengths.

- Design of micro-insurance products must have the features of simplicity, availability, affordability, accessibility and flexibility.

The Committee studied four different models for delivering micro-insurance services to the targeted clientele, viz., the Partner-Agent Model, Full Service Model, Community Based Model and Provider Model.

Leveraging the Existing Network for Micro-Insurance

To economise on costs and to increase the outreach of micro-insurance to the poor, the insurers need to utilize existing Government organisations and NGOs, having greater acceptability among the financially excluded. The partner-agent model for delivery where the insurer underwrites the risk and the distribution is handled by an existing intermediary, seems apt in this scenario.

Linking Micro Credit with Micro Insurance

The Committee concurs with the view that offering microcredit without micro-insurance is financial behaviour fraught with risk. There is, therefore, a need to emphasise linking of microcredit with micro-insurance.

Further, as it helps in bringing down the inherent risk cost of lending, the Committee feels that NABARD should be regularly involved in issues relating to rural and micro insurance to leverage on its experience of being a catalyst in the field of microcredit.

Implementation Strategy for Micro-Insurance

The Committee has identified major areas for formulation of strategies for effective implementation of micro-insurance programmes as explained in the following paragraphs:

Human Resources Requirement and Training

To tap the huge micro-insurance potential, IRDA may consider putting in place an appropriate institutional structure for deciding on service packages including premia and formulating strategies for effective promotion of micro-insurance. There is also a felt need for development, of both full-time and part-time staff, thru' effective training in insurance marketing and servicing concepts.

Operations and Systems

To address the requirements of the huge market potential available, appropriate systems should be evolved for tracking client information, either manually or using technology. While a technology platform may take time for setting up, in the long-run, the same will be cost-effective and reliable. Similarly, the procedures for claims, premium payments / renewals and other services should be formalized along with increased customization of products to stimulate demand.

Development of Adequate Feedback Mechanism

Keeping in view the diverse nature of market requirements, suitable mechanisms to collect market intelligence, collating and interpretation of the same in a formally structured manner, is important for product development and process refinement.

Development of Data Base

High costs of penetration and acquisition often leads to higher pricing of products, thereby impacting client outreach and market depth. Building up historical data base on risk profiles, claims, settlement ratios, etc., will facilitate in better pricing of products, based on actual rather than presumed risks. Besides enabling cost reduction, warehousing of such data will make the market more transparent for entry of more operators.

Consumer Education, Marketing and Grievance Handling

The micro-insurance sector is unique in the sense that there is an ongoing challenge to explain the concept and benefits to the insured. Creating awareness thru' use of pictorial posters, local folk arts and street theatres might be useful to explain the mechanisms of insurance. Local community-based organisations could organize premium collections, as they have better access to the local people. To make it more acceptable to the people, micro-insurance products, apart from covering only risks, should also provide an opportunity for long term savings (endowment).

Product Development/Process Re-engineering

Customised product development to suit the varying requirements of the local populace is a pre-requisite. The processes/procedures are to be streamlined and simplified, to facilitate easier access for the rural poor. Information should be made available in vernacular for easy understanding of the terms on offer.

Using Existing Infrastructure

Micro-insurance service providers can use the existing banking infrastructure and also adopt the agency-mode (NGOs, SHGs, NBFCs, etc.) for providing services, thereby leveraging on the existing physical branch network and reducing costs.

Use of Technology

The technology platforms being envisioned to facilitate financial inclusion should enable micro-insurance transactions also. Towards this end, there is a need to integrate the various modules - savings, credit, insurance, etc. - into the technology framework so that holistic inclusive efforts are possible in the rural areas.

Review of Existing Schemes

There are a large number of group life and health insurance schemes which are run by various central ministries and State Governments. The level of actual coverage in terms of claims preferred and settled in such schemes is disturbingly low. These schemes should be reviewed by an expert group set up by the IRDA.

Life Insurance:

A wide range of products are available but penetration is

really limited in rural areas. The procedural requirements at the time of entry and in case of claims settlement are cumbersome. The commission structure for agents is also heavily weighed in favour of getting new policies with very little incentive to service existing policies. In this regard, Micro Insurance Guidelines (MIG) 2005 issued by IRDA has provided for equal commission throughout the life of a policy and this will now remove the disincentive in servicing existing policy holders.

Health Insurance*:*

In case of Health Insurance, penetration level is even much lower than Life Insurance. The two categories viz., Critical Illness and Hospitalisation are the main product segments. Some State Governments have developed Health Insurance schemes which are still in very early stages.

The Committee has observed that the mutual health insurance models have advantages of its members performing a number of roles such as awareness creation, marketing, enrolment, premium collection, claims processing, monitoring, etc. Under this arrangement, the costs of offering small-ticket health insurance gets significantly reduced. The high co-variant risks such as epidemics will have to be taken care of by a mutual entity taking re-insurance for such risks.

IRDA has also suggested that the capital requirements for stand-alone health insurance companies be reduced to Rs.50 crore as against Rs.100 crore for Life Insurance Companies and the Committee endorses the same.

Crop Insurance*:*

This is a very important risk mitigation arrangement for small and marginal farmers. However, leaving the discretion to notify crops/regions to state governments has contributed to adverse selection. Further, claims settlement based on yield estimation has been cumbersome and the sampling area for crop cutting experiments is very large. An alternative model based on weather insurance has been attempted.

To make it more effective, there is a need for having a

large number of smaller weather stations. The Committee recommends that policies be evolved to make crop insurance universal, viz., applicable to all crops/regions and pricing actuarial.

Livestock Insurance*:*

As in Life Insurance, the problem lies in the process of enrolment and claims settlement. Several pilots indicate that the involvement of local organisations like SHGs, dairy co-operatives, NGOs and MFIs improves the quality of service, reduces false claims and expedites claims settlement. The Committee recommends that these experiences be studied and adopted by insurance companies.

Asset Insurance*:*

This could cover a wide range including residential buildings, farm and non-farm equipments and vehicles. The main constraint seems to be lack of distribution channels appropriate for lower income groups. The Committee again recommends that involving local NGOs, MFIs, SHGs, etc. as distribution channels as well as facilitators of claims settlements would be quite useful.

Demand Side Causes and Solutions for Financial Inclusion

The Committee's Report has so far concentrated on supply side issues of financial inclusion and what can be done to enhance supply of financial services, through increased outreach by existing institutions, enhancing their incentives to serve the excluded and adding new distribution channels. The Committee is of the view that financial exclusion is also caused by demand side issues. Unless some initiatives are taken on the demand side, or in the "real sectors", mere supply side solutions from the financial sector will not work.

Recommendations: Human Development

Regions, segments and sectors financially excluded require substantial investments in human development. In particular, primary health, nutrition, primary education and vocational training need attention. The Twelfth Finance Commission had already taken a lead in this direction by earmarking additional funds for health and education in backward States. The Committee is of the view that this will lead to enhanced economic efficiency and consequent demand for financial inclusion, within a few years.

Access to Land and Titling

The Committee is supportive of various Government programmes under which surplus land is distributed to landless and marginal farmers. The Committee has also noted that the Government has enacted recently The Forest Dwellers and Tribal Land Rights Act, 2006, which will ensure that those who had been cultivating a piece of land for decades in the middle of forests, will now get security of tenure. This will open up the possibility of their accessing credit from banks.

The Committee has noted and endorses the recent move by NABARD to provide refinance for credit extended by banks and co-operatives to oral lessees and tenant farmers. This category of farmers has long been financially excluded due to lack of land titling or recorded tenures. Procedural changes in banks must be brought about to extend credit outreach to all such productive farmers.

Banks hesitate to finance tenant farmers / oral lessees as they do not have documentary proof of their right to till the land for raising crops or for investment purposes. Recording of tenancy and ownership rights on land is an important measure to enable access to credit.

Certificates by revenue officers or a system of land cultivation certificate by the Village Panchayats or local bodies may be made acceptable as documentary proof for cultivating the land.

Computerisation of land records will lead to systematization of land records and overall availability of required information to banks facilitating their loan appraisal process. It is observed that 12 States have already initiated the process and GoI may advise all States to give priority for completing this process within a year. This will reduce cost to farmers in obtaining various documents and recording encumbrance.

Access to Work: NREGA

Given the fact that nearly 80% of farmer households in the country are small and marginal farmers, who rarely have work on their own farms for more than 100 days a year, the availability of wage employment in the vicinity of their villages is critical. In this context the Committee noted the nation-wide roll-out plans supported by the National Rural Employment Guarantee Act (NREGA) which ensures that every household in need can ask for paid wage work for up to 100 days per year.

The Committee endorses the creative use of the NREGP payments thru' bank accounts to enhance financial inclusion, as practiced in Andhra Pradesh. In Andhra Pradesh, the beneficiaries/depositors will be issued smart cards to enable transactions at several locations besides the bank branch.

Infrastructure Support

The Committee noted the significant progress made for rural connectivity through the Pradhan Mantri Gram Sadak Yojana and the attempt to extend electric power to unconnected villages through the Rajiv Gandhi Gram Vidyutikaran Yojana. In several states the RIDF managed by NABARD has enabled the creation of much needed roads, bridges, irrigation canals, water harvesting structures and other useful infrastructure. The Committee endorses this and recommends a further impetus in the area.

The National Development Council (NDC) has recommended that the normative allocation of RIDF funds among States should be decided by factoring in, *inter alia*, the CD ratio as a relevant criterion. This should be attempted by NABARD to improve equitable distribution of RIDF resources.

Enhancing Productivity and Incomes

Productivity Enhancement

In this connection, the Committee has already recommended the establishment of Nodal Branches in each block to undertake intensive efforts for agricultural and business development services to farm and non-farm sector borrowers respectively. The Committee also recommends that banks explore tie-ups with government extension agencies, Krishi Vigyan Kendras, reputed NGOs working in this field, agri-business clinics and corporates engaged in agricultural activities, to provide inputs, extension services and market linkages to the bank's borrowers so as to offer credit plus services and enhance the efficiency of credit.

Value Addition: Primary Processing

The Committee recommends that efforts should be made to ensure that all agricultural produce is subjected to primary and if possible secondary value addition locally. This means that post-harvest drying, sorting, grading and packing, can be done at the village level, preferably by women's SHGs. Farmers groups can come together to establish secondary value addition facilities such as groundnut shelling, cotton ginning, dal milling, rice hulling, fruit pulping, milk chilling, etc.

Alternate Market Linkages

Roads, transport, power and water provide critical linkages in support of production-based activities. Social services like health, education, etc. contribute to improvements in the quality of rural life. State Governments should prioritise infrastructure planning, use of funds of the National Rural Employment Guarantee Programme (NREGP) for building critical infrastructure and encourage community participation in creation and maintenance of assets.

Reducing Vulnerability

Risk Mitigation through Non-financial Channels

A vast majority of poorer households in India are exposed to high levels of risk and considered as not insurable at reasonable levels of premium. Their risk levels need to be mitigated through soil and water conservation measures, watershed development, installing protective irrigation and by using appropriate agronomic practices all the way from ploughing techniques to seed selection and timely farm operations. In the case of livestock rearers, risks can be reduced by proper herd management practices and mass vaccination for example against foot and mouth disease. It is only after these type of investments have reduced the risks in farming that the private expense in buying insurance can be affordable.

Calamity Relief Fund

Repeated natural calamities and consequent rescheduling of bank loans take the debt burden beyond the repaying capacity of farmers. There is a need for the creation of a National Calamity Fund to address the problems of farmers in distress districts. Further, the subsidy on crop insurance may be directed more effectively towards the disadvantaged sectors.

Managing Price Risks through Warehouse Receipts and Commodity Derivatives

Apart from the physical risks which impact crop yields, farmers also suffer from price risks. In bumper years, their harvest fetches low prices. In order to hedge against such price risks the right instrument is commodity derivatives, particularly futures options in which a farmer can be assured of selling his produce at a certain price in future.

The Committee also noted that the Indian farmer is highly attuned to dealing in spot markets, traditionally known as Mandis, where the commodity is exchanged for cash. The

Committee therefore supports any initiatives towards improving the transactional efficiency of spot markets.

The Committee noted that several multi-commodity exchanges have come up in the last few years and that they are registering a large turn over. This enables farmers to discover the future price and take decisions related to crop selection. The Committee is supportive of such initiatives.

However, the Committee noted the fact that a vast majority of financially excluded farmers have only a small marketable surplus and thus cannot benefit from the vibrant commodity exchanges, where the minimum traded lot is much larger than what the individual farmer has to offer. In order to extend the benefits of derivative exchanges to excluded farmers, aggregation mechanisms such as cooperatives need to come up.

In the interim, financial instruments such as warehouse receipts and post-harvest credit can be offered so that farmers can avoid distress sales. The passage of the Warehousing (Development and Regulation) Bill, 2005 by Parliament is likely to open up a number of avenues for farmers to mitigate their price risks by encashing stock pledged in a warehouse to meet their cash needs, while waiting for the right price. The Committee is supportive of efforts to establish a chain of authorized warehouses throughout rural India, to provide such services, particularly when such warehouses are linked to PACS.

Organising the Unorganised Producers

In order for financial inclusion efforts to be sustainable, banks need to aggregate credit demand from the small borrowers. The celebrated mechanism for this is the SHG of which there are now more than 2.9 million in India linked with banks.

Another well known mechanism for collective action is commodity cooperatives. There is no better example than the dairy producers cooperative societies established by the

NDDB.

The Committee recommends the establishment of similar commodity cooperatives to cover a large number of small and marginal producers all over the country. The effort for bringing the producers together can be undertaken by specialized agencies like NDDB and suitable NGOs, while the cost for this should be defrayed by either the Government or by the banks, or a combination thereof.

The Financial Inclusion Fund cannot be used for a better purpose than supporting a competent and committed agency to organise commodity producer cooperatives in areas such as large cardamom in Sikkim, lac in tribal areas of Eastern Madhya Pradesh, Tasar in Northern Jharkand and seaweed in coastal Andhra Pradesh.

The Committee endorses Government programmes such as *Velugu programme* in Andhra Pradesh, which promote organizing the unorganized producers, and recognizes that this cannot happen without the social intermediate of competent and committed NGOs. The legitimate expenses of such intermerdiaries need to be met. Initially, banks can lend to groups based on considerations of viability; but this will eventually lead to individual lending as individual producers grow. This is the slow and steady process that the Committee recommends to build true financial inclusion.

Bibliography

Bibliography

Ahluwalia, Montek Singh (1996): 'New Economic Policy and Agriculture: Some Reflections', Inaugural address delivered at the 55th Annual Conference of Indian Society of Agricultural Economics held at Institute of Rural Management, Anand (Gujarat) on November 2, 1995, published in Indian Journal of Agricultural Economics, Vol. 51, No. 3, July-September.

Alagh. K.Y. (1998-99): 'Agricultural Trade and Policies', The Indian Economic Journal, Jan-Mar, Vol. 46, No. 3, p. 56.

Balakrishnan (2000): *Agriculture and Economic Reforms, Growth and Welfare*, EPW, Vol. 35, No. 12

Damodaram A., *WTO, Agriculture Agreement, Common Property Resources and Income Diversification Strategy*, EPW, September 22, 2001.

Deaton, A. and Jean Dreze (2002): *Poverty and Inequality in India: A Re-examination*, Economic and Political Weekly (EPW), September 7, 2002.

Dreze, Jean and A. Sen (2002): 'India: Development and Participation', Oxford University Press.

Government of India, *Agricultural Statistics at a Glance 2002*, Agricultural Statistics Division, Ministry of Agriculture and Co-operation, New Delhi.

——*Economic Survey* (Various Years).

——Planning Commission, *Eighth Five Year Plan* (1992-97), Vol. I.

——Planning Commission, *Ninth Five Year Plan* (1997-2002), Volumes I and II.

——Planning Commission, *Seventh Five Year Plan* (1985-90), Vol. II.

——Planning Commission, *Sixth Five Year Plan* (1980-85).

——Planning Commission, *Tenth Five Year Plan* (2002-07), Volumes I and II.

Gulati Ashok (1998), *Indian Agriculture in an Open Economy: Will it Prosper?* in Isher Judge Ahluwalia and I.M.D. Little, 'India's Economic Reforms and Development: Essays for Manmohan Singh', Oxford University Press, New Delhi.

International Agricultural Trade Research Consortium (IATRC); *The Uruguay Round Agreement on Agriculture: An Evaluation*; IATRC Commissioned Paper No. 9. St. Paul, Minn.: IATRC., 1994

Jha, D. 2001: 'Agriculture Research and Small Farmers', Presidential Address, 60th Annual Conference of Indian Society of Agricultural Economics. Institute for Studies in Population, Agricultural and Rural Change, University of Kalyani, Kalyani.

Kishore Kumar, N and Shehana, R.S, *WTO Accord vis-à-vis Indian Scenario,* Kissan World, July 19, 2000.

Konar, D.N. (1997): 'Trend of Indian Agriculture in the Post Independence Period', Artha Beekha, Vol. 6, No. 2, December.

Krishna, Raj and G.S. Raychaudhuri (1980): 'Some Aspects of Wheat and Rice Price Policy in India', World Bank Staff Working Paper No. 381, April (Washington, DC: The World Bank).

Kumar, P., *Agricultural Performance and Productivity*, in S.S. Acharya and D.P. Chaudhri, Indian Agricultural Policy at the Crossroads: Priorities and Agenda. Rawat Publications, Jaipur and New Delhi.

Ministry of Commerce & Industry and Ministry of Agriculture (2001) *WTO Agreement on Agriculture: India's Proposals.*

Ministry of Commerce, *India and the WTO,* newsletter, Various issues.

Nayyar, Deepak and Sen, Abhijit, *International Trade and the Agricultural Sector in India*, Economic and Political Weekly (EPW), May 14, 1994.

Parikh, Kirit S., N.S.S. Narayana, Manoj K. Panda and A. Ganesh Kumar (1996): *Strategies for Agricultural*

Liberalisation: Consequences for Growth, Welfare and Distribution, mimeo, Indira Gandhi Institute of Development Research, Mumbai.

Rao Hanumantha C.H. (1995), *Liberalization of Agriculture in India - Some Major Issues*, Indian Journal of Agricultural Economics, Vol. No.3.

Rao, C.H. Hanumantha and Ashok Gulati (1994): *Indian Agriculture: Emerging Perspectives and Policy Issues*, Economic and Political Weekly (EPW), Review of Agriculture, Vol. XXXI (53), 31st December.

Rao, Hanumantha C.H. (1999), *Changing Economic Structure of the Rural Economy in Asia and the Pacific,* paper presented at the study meeting on Rural Transformation, held at Yogakarta, Indonesia, November 29 to December 3.

Rao, Hanumantha C. H. (2003): *Reform Agenda for Agriculture*, Economic and Political Weekly (EPW), Vol. 8, No. 7.

Rao, Hanumantha C.H. (2001): *WTO and Viability of Indian Agriculture*", Economic and Political Weekly (EPW), September 8, 2001.

Reserve Bank of India, *Bulletin (various issues).*

——*Handbook of Statistics on Indian Economy* (various years)

——*Report on Currency and Finance* (various years).

Sawant, S.D., V. Daptardar, S. Mhatre (2002): *Capital Formation and Growth in Agriculture - Neglected Aspects and Dimensions*, Economic and Political Weekly (EPW), March 16, 2002.

Sengupta, K. (1991): *Procurement Prices and Inflation*, Yojana, October, Vol. 35 New Delhi.

Sharma Pardeep & Gulati Ashok (1995): *WTO and Indian Agriculture*, Economic and Political Weekly (EPW), March 10.

Sharma, U.S. (1988): *Decentralized Planning Model for Rural Development,* Nirnay, March.

Shetty, S.L. (2003): *Credit Flows to Rural Poor*, mimeo, EPW Research Foundation, Mumbai.

Singh Rakesh (2000): *An Assessment of Agriportals in India*, Discussion Paper, NMIMS, December.

Subramanian, Shankar (1993): *Agricultural Trade Liberalisation and India* (Paris: Development Centre Studies, OECD).

Thamarajakshi, R (1999): *Agriculture and Economic Reforms,* Economic and Political Weekly (EPW), Vol. 34, No. 33.

Timothy Josling, *Agricultural Trade Policy: Completing the Reform*, Institute for International Economics, 1998.

Vaidyananthan, A. (2000): *Indian Agriculture Policy,* Economic and Political Weekly (EPW), Vol.35 No. 10.

Vyas, V.S. (2001): *Agriculture - Second round of Economic Reforms*, Economic and Political Weekly (EPW), Vol. 36, No. 10.

Vyas, V.S., *WTO and Indian Agriculture,* Agricultural Science Section, at the 88th Session of the Indian Science Congress, Indian Agricultural Research Institute, New Delhi.

World Bank (2003): *India: Sustaining Reform, Reducing Poverty,* A World Bank Development Policy Review, Oxford University Press.

Index

Index